Twelfth Night

Dr Stevie Davies lectured in English Literature at Manchester University from 1971 to 1984. She left to become a full-time novelist and literary critic. Her novel, *Boy Blue*, published in 1987, won the Fawcett Society Book Prize in 1989, and was followed by *Primavera* (1990), *Arms and the Girl* (1992) and *Closing the Book* (1994). She has published eleven critical books, the most recent being *John Donne* (1994), *Emily Brontë: Heretic* (1994) and *Henry Vaughan* (1995). She has written three books in the Penguin Critical Studies series; *To the Lighthouse*, *Twelfth Night* and *The Taming of the Shrew*, and her edition of *The Tenant of Wildfell Hall* is forthcoming in Penguin Classics. She is currently Senior Research Fellow at Roehampton Institute.

CW00954334

Penguin Critical Studies
Advisory Editor: Bryan Loughrey

William Shakespeare

Twelfth Night

Stevie Davies

Penguin Books

PENGUIN BOOKS

Published by the Penguin Group
Penguin Books Ltd, 27 Wrights Lane, London W8 5TZ, England
Penguin Books USA Inc., 375 Hudson Street, New York, New York 10014, USA
Penguin Books Australia Ltd, Ringwood, Victoria, Australia
Penguin Books Canada Ltd, 10 Alcorn Avenue, Toronto, Ontario, Canada M4V 3B2
Penguin Books (NZ) Ltd, 182–190 Wairau Road, Auckland 10, New Zealand

Penguin Books Ltd, Registered Offices: Harmondsworth, Middlesex, England

First published 1993
10 9 8 7 6 5 4 3

Typeset by Datix International Limited, Bungay, Suffolk
Filmset in 9/11 pt Monophoto Times New Roman
Printed in England by Clays Ltd, St Ives plc

To Frank

So are you to my thoughts
  as food to life

Contents

Acknowledgements

My thanks are due to Andrew Howdle, whose beautiful paintings on Elizabethan themes gave a vivid imaginative background to my writing; to Rosalie Wilkins for her constant and loving encouragement; to Beth Brownhill and Margaret Argyle for the support of their friendship; to my editor, Bryan Loughrey, for his patience and understanding; and especially to my husband, Frank Regan, for his care and support during the illness which interrupted the composition of the book – and for putting me back together again so that I could resume and complete the work in good time.

Introduction: The Critic's Lament

'Our disputes,' wrote Montaigne in his essay 'On Experience', 'are about words.' But words, as Feste observes in *Twelfth Night*, are rascals. They exhibit the supple reversibility of a fine leather glove, able to be turned inside-out and outside-in well-nigh simultaneously. This two-faced rascality of words is compounded by their refusal to be defined by any measure except their own slippery fraternity:

VIOLA   *Thy reason, man?*
FESTE   *Troth, sir, I can yield you none without words, and words are grown so false, I am loath to prove reason with them.*

(III.1.21–4)

Later, Bacon in *The Advancement of Learning* would express a similar awareness of the self-reflexive ambivalence of language, whose voluptuous semantic excess was in flagrant breach of reason and exactitude. Montaigne's point was slightly different: his was, in essence, an objection to the interpretation of already existent and satisfactory texts. Having observed the monstrous accumulation through history of words explaining other words, interpretations of interpretations of interpretations, Montaigne felt a grotesque disparity between any original work and the critical commentaries that aspired to explain it; say, between the play *Twelfth Night* and a book which claims to interpret or explain it. Any word which is substituted for another is an alloy of similarity to and difference from the original; its vagrant suggestions are not only irrelevant but lead to further irrelevances, moving inevitably and anarchically away from the initial topic:

I ask what is Nature, Pleasure, a Circle, and Substitution. The question is couched in words, and is answered in the same coin. A stone is a body. But if you press the point: And what is a body? – A substance. – And what is a substance? and so on, you will end by driving the answerer to exhaust his dictionary. One substitutes one word for another that is often less well understood . . .
. . . We put one question and receive a hive full in return. As no event and no shape entirely resembles another, so none is wholly different from another. An ingenious mixture on nature's part! If our faces were not similar, we could not distinguish a man from a beast; if they were not dissimilar, we could not distinguish one man from another. All things hold together by some similarity;

every example limps; and the comparison which is derived from experience is always weak and imperfect; yet comparisons always join at one corner or another.

(Montaigne, *Essays*, pp. 349–50)

If to explain is to falsify, since only the original words maintain their exact meaning and all linguistic substitutions simply multiply arbitrary nuances, the literary critic joins Shakespeare's Clown as a 'corrupter of words' (III.1.34–5). What is *Twelfth Night*? – A comedy. – And what is a comedy? – A play upon words. – And what are words? – Words are only ever words. Montaigne's mirror reveals the face of the commentator as that of an arrogant fool. But *Twelfth Night*, with its multiple equivocations, ironies, mirrorings and the light, fugitive texture of its wit, is a quintessential text for proving the critic's folly. Its central motif of identical twins reproduces the freak factor which, in Montaigne's analysis, confounds the verbal and social order, which depends on a mating of resemblance with difference in the sign-system: 'if [our faces] were not dissimilar, we could not distinguish one man from another'. Identical twins in the linguistic world (one symbol, two meanings) are puns. In the dazzling scintillations of likeness in difference and difference in likeness which *Twelfth Night* presents, language is a quicksilver medium defying scholarly annotation as pomposity and exegesis as Malvolian narcissism.

The text of this as of any play written for the theatre is essentially unstable – but perhaps *Twelfth Night* more than most. I do not mean this in the bibliographical sense, for we have more or less agreed a definitive version, bar a few commas and colons. But the written text of a play is, by its very nature, incomplete: at once disembodied and static. Around the speeches on the page opens an immeasurable and silent blankness which the actors must fill with presence, gesture, movement. Malleable faces and fluid gestures must pick up those half-significant cues, the words on the page, and negotiate them into significance by transforming them into aspects of embodied action. In so doing, they will automatically consign them to time. So the critic's activity is not even secondary but tertiary, since it must defer to the primacy of the drama as performance-art and, in the case of *Twelfth Night*, performance-art which takes as its own central topics performance and art. The acting of this play about acting is its truer interpretation, rather than the critic's lucubrations. But performance itself is various and variable, not only from director to director, age to age, but even from night to night. *Twelfth Night* contains multitudinous *Twelfth Night*s and the dormant seeds of many more, whether generated by a producer's singular comprehensive reading of the text or the nuanced particularities of the actors' voices. On the Elizabethan stage, the women's and cross-dressing women's parts were taken by boys, so that stage-conditions radically affected the experience of gender, another central theme of the play. The implications of sexual ambiguity might, under these conditions, be diametrically opposite to those feminist suggestions reflected in the modern custom of having a 'real' woman play Viola/'Cesario'. The longer one peruses these ambivalences, not to mention the seven different ways Sir Toby might deliver himself of the phrase 'Tilly-vally!' or, more crucially, Malvolio affirm that 'I think nobly of the soul . . .', the more one registers this play of shimmering paradox as a thing that cannot be known save in its own language as 'A natural perspective, that is and is not' (V.1.214). My reaction to such disparity, for the purposes of this book, has been to stress it in the context of a reading which seeks to sustain lines of intelligible argument while being recurrently haunted by the remembered or imagined voices of acted interpretations. In 'Of Experience', Montaigne went on to assess the status of utterances in a pregnant phrase: 'A speech belongs half to the speaker, half to him who hears it.' The concept of joint ownership of meaning at least encourages the listener-reader to affirm with conviction her own half-truths.

But the listener in the auditorium is not the same person as the reader. A further irritant for the critic comes of the difficulty of bridging the gap between the ponderousness of the studious reading-experience and the lightness or levity of the theatrical experience of this comedy. The one weighs every scruple of every word, but the eye returns again and again to add mass and allusion to passages which stand out for the reader with an especial pointedness; the other *has* completed this activity of weighing every word prior to performance, but is obliged to commit each to the evanescence of the chronologically passing moment. Thus the reading-experience may often be unbalanced, piling some lines, which seem 'important' with graver significance than others, for as the eye flicks to and fro in the text, so the memory supplies the mind with the echo of earlier speeches, and there is time to pause and analyse. All such activity literally stops the play; it does an interfering injustice to its action, which exists in time, and must keep time. In taking these liber-ties, the reading-experience tends to sacrifice comedy to what I shall call, for want of a better word, resonance. The critic finds more to think and talk about in great lyric speeches, for instance, than in the light, artfully casual exchanges which are the essence of *Twelfth Night* as a theatrical event. Thus the critic gives greater weight to Viola's 'willow cabin' speech (I.5.257 ff.) and her 'Patience on a monument' passage (II.4.109 ff.) than to some of the funniest (and therefore, dramatically richest) lines in the play. What, for instance, is the critic to say about Malvolio's immortal, 'Sweet lady! Ho! Ho!' (II.4.17). Polysyllabically encumbered as we are, we creak in heavy boots as quietly as possible around the numerous awkward instances of material which leave us speechless, hoping not to be detected. 'Yes;' riposte Malvolio later in the same scene, 'nightingales answer daws' (III.4.34): it is one of the play's most glorious lines in its loftily fatuous snootiness, but there is nothing very much to be said about it. In the theatre, every line exacts, if not its due weight, at least a chance to be heard, and in this respect the dramatic experience is generally more democratic in reproducing, once round, without replaying, the whole play. Performance relates all temporally and temporarily as part of a process, so that the language and the experience it mediates derive from all that has gone before and flow into what is to come. To think and write about *Twelfth Night* we have to cut slices and deny the seamless temporality of the dramatic process. Standing back from the sequential reading-process, we tend to fix it into representative iconic tableaux or a series of poetic passages which seem to crystallize what the play means to us. This, of course, is also true of the audience, going home after the play: the fluent extemporaneousness which is the play's illusion, with its unfolding of colour, light, music, motion and talk, is reduced to a handful of static pictures which act as mnemonics of the production. We can never wholly 'remember' the play we saw. The Clown's Song which ends *Twelfth Night* is conclusive: 'But that's all one, our play is done, / And we'll strive to please you every day' (V.1.404–5). With these words, this liminal figure, midway between character and actor, between the play's vaporous action and everyday actuality, closes down the comedy, reminding us that it is essentially a closed form, of the passing moment, at most a finite recurrence (if you'll pay for another ticket tomorrow).

It may be objected that such gaps as I am describing between acted text and deliberative utterance have no especial pertinence to *Twelfth Night*, being generally true of all drama. But my experience of writing this critical study suggests that Montaigne's falsification-factor comes more fully into play in reading and explicating *Twelfth Night* than in other major works. To reflect upon why this is so is to understand something essential about the play. It cannot be made to function readily as 'closet drama', where the reader's mind is stage, cast, director and audience. The poetic and philosophical monumentality of, say, *King Lear*, are such that Charles Lamb believed that it could not be performed convincingly on a stage, for only the imagination could do justice to its sublimity and scale. Even if you do not take that extreme point of view, you can see how it functions as dramatic poem as well as poetic drama; a meditation-piece of profound dimensions. The scholar can be happy with such a text, for her discourse is, or can be made to seem, at home with it. In comedy the intelligent, fencing wit and problematic serio-comic structure of *Much Ado About Nothing* give ample space for elucidation: the play does not usually make a fool of the commentator. But *Twelfth Night* is all fools and fooling, from the ninny to the apparent maniac, the fantasist to the sot. As a piece of festive entertainment, it is in large part adults' child's play. And as its beauty is fugitive and diaphanous, so its wit, airy or rowdy, belongs to the perishable theatrical moment and dies with exposure, as Maria says of the 'device' which may 'take air, and taint' (III.4.130–31). There is a quality in *Twelfth Night* which candour compels me to describe as pure silliness: a silliness, rather, which is pure in the theatre, and the very essence of the audience's enjoyment. No critic can feel comfortable with silliness, for one has a natural objection to seeming implicated. *Twelfth Night* is an embarrassing play. So aware of pompous and posturing follies, it is none-too-merciful to offenders in this kind: Olivia squirmingly blushes to the roots of her hair as she presses her ardent case upon the reluctant youth (III.1.108 ff.); Malvolio converts his blush to red-hot ire (V.1.300 ff.); Viola winces and fidgets in the embarrassing fiction of her doublet and hose (III.4.222 ff.). The Fool's revolving mirror gleams and winks at foolhardy characters, audience and critics alike. We link the play to tribal initiation-rites, with their middle-stage of identity-loss and confusion (Edward Berry, *Shakespeare's Comic Rites*); to Renaissance humanist views of metamorphosis (William C. Carroll, *Metamorphosis of Shakespeare's Comedy*); to the structure of Elizabethan holiday (C. L. Barber, *Shakespeare's Festive Comedy*); to theories of comedy as social corrective, the 'Wise Fool' tradition, Renaissance musicology, 'feminist' cross-dressing, satire on Petrarchan love-conventions – and there is always something missing, or fractionally 'out'. Dr Johnson skewered it neatly in his dismissive comment on *Twelfth Night* as a mere divertimento which 'fails to produce the proper instruction required in the drama, as it exhibits no just picture of life' (Edition of *The Works of William Shakespear*, 1765). Surely Dr Johnson was reacting to the silliness of *Twelfth Night*, its surface mirth which may also be called its soul, and pointing out that this lifts it away from the world of serious discourse, to float in the ether of its own aestheticism and laughter. *Twelfth Night* has nothing solid to teach us.

However, if silliness were all, there would be no problem; we should not itch to write about this comedy, to mark and fix it with our ink. The real trick is to link the play's flighty refusal of the burden of gravity to the deeper dreams, poignancies and swirling human conflicts it glimmeringly reflects. For paradoxically, the play is like a sheen or gloss upon some very harsh, dark themes. It considers bereavement, strandedness and absence; the failure of desire and insight; self-delusion and loss of identity; class conflict and cruelty. But it makes these reflections in a guilefully mellifluous or tickling way, combining the comic romance medium and the spellbinding lyric voice to produce an anodyne effect – that is, if you accept and respond to the sugary placebo of *Twelfth Night*'s incomparable blend of humour and beauty. From the earliest scenes we suspect, and soon know for sure, that the apparently dead may be only hidden; the love-lorn are not hurting so very much. For the play is self-consciously an artifice throughout, dwelling on role-play, conventions, costume, script, actors and acting, musical entertainment, the 'let's pretend' of the theatre with its whole bag of tricks on show. This aestheticism and self-reflexiveness seem to offer a way of connecting the ambivalent, protean surfaces of *Twelfth Night* with the haunting depths they imply but do not denote. The critic's problem is to find a language capable of suggesting the 'sea-change / Into something rich and strange' (*The Tempest* (I.2.401–2)) of the refracted, resolving light cast on sad or stressful facts by comic perception.

In my first chapter, using the principles elucidated in Emrys Jones's *Scenic Form in Shakespeare* (a classic work which mediates between the reader of the texts and the acted plays as unfolding processes on the stage), I offer an introductory account (Act by Act) of the dramatic action, rhythm and dynamics of *Twelfth Night*. A second chapter considers the meaning of the play in terms of its musicality and aestheticism, and a brief discussion of the 'Folly' tradition (Chapter 3) leads into a chapter on the language of *Twelfth Night* and *Twelfth Night* as a play about language, which consciously incorporates the Montaignian and Baconian criticisms of language that have plagued this Introduction. In Chapter 5, Malvolio – or rather, several Malvolios – and his persecutors wrestle, and I elaborate a 'Puritan' reading of his character and function. The embarrassing gap between the reading- and the watching-experience is brought into relief in this chapter, which ponders the meanness of practical jokes, together with their licensing of prejudice. The final chapter dwells on the problematics of sexuality in *Twelfth Night*, rejecting a 'feminist' interpretation in favour of a reading which sees the homoerotic suggestions of the acted play as primary, both in the Elizabethan theatre of boy-actors and on the modern stage. Relating the figures of Viola/'Cesario' to the Young Man of Shakespeare's Sonnets and the aggrieved and solitary Antonio to the poetic persona of the sequence, I end where I began, with Montaigne, this time his gossip about the relationship between the fantasizing imagination and sex-change. Shakespeare, who had read Montaigne in his friend John Florio's translation of 1595, shared the essayist's conviction of the hair-raising potency of the human imagination.

Twelfth Night plays about with hermeneutics – the art of interpretation. Its people are presented as texts to be read, construed and expounded, but the readers bring to this exercise a distorting lens whose convexities or concavities are ground to the wanton measure of individual surmise and desire. They over-read or under-read the signs on the page of the human face and tongue. Olivia 'reads' the text of Viola's message as a provocation to love. Understandably, she can make neither head nor tail of Malvolio's simpering addresses, for these in turn are based on an interpretation of an aberrant text (the letter she never wrote). The Fool interprets the text of Malvolio's letter in Act V by reading it in a manic voice. Viola, as her master's messenger-boy, interprets his ardour to Olivia's greedy and ravished ear, to exuberant but disastrous effect. Excess of meaning abounds and breeds in her heady elaboration of Orsino's passion, in the crucial Act I, scene 5. The higher the mutual delight of Viola and Olivia in their verbal fencing soars, the further the original subject is left behind. Viola's interpretation leads inexorably away from what it is duty-bound to interpret:

> OLIVIA ... *Where lies your text?*
> VIOLA *In Orsino's bosom.*
> OLIVIA *In his bosom! In what chapter of his bosom?*
> VIOLA *To answer by the method, in the first of his heart.*
> OLIVIA *O, I have read it; it is heresy.*
>
> (I.5.214–18)

The search for a text of *Twelfth Night* to interpret leads to a labyrinth of possibilities: an account of a recent production at which one happened to be present; a reconstructed version of what the Elizabethan audience saw; a composite of remembered and imagined versions; a purely mental construct formed by reading and rereading; a mingling of the reading-experience and acted versions. Maybe it is always true that the text lies in miscellaneous chapters of one's bosom – chapters which tell different truths. *Twelfth Night* has a singular ability to shift and dissolve, the longer the critic strains to fix it with her eye, assuming a way-ward ambivalence in keeping with the *trompe-l'oeil* illusionism of the play's manner, with its shot-silk mind 'of changeable taffeta', 'a very opal', as Feste says of Orsino. For Charles Lamb, the problem of the authoritative text stabilized when you took up 'that vantage-ground of abstraction which reading possesses over seeing' ('On The Tragedies of Shakespeare', p. 31). But Lamb's quarrel was with acted versions of tragedy, rather than comedy, which lives most fully in the staged moment rather than the studious imagination. In the theatre, seeing is not only believing, but understanding.

1. Sources and Scenic Development

At our feast wee had a play called 'Twelve Night, or What You Will', much like the Commedy of Errores, or Menechmi in Plautus, but most like and neere to that in Italian called *Inganni*. A good practise in it to make the Steward beleeve his Lady widdowe was in love with him, by counterfeyting a letter as from his Lady in generall terms, telling him what shee liked best in him, and prescribing his gesture in smiling, his apparaile, etc., and then when he came to practise making him beleeve they took him to be mad.

(Palmer, D. J. (ed.), *'Twelfth Night': A Casebook*, p. 25)

Smarmily smiling and astonishing his Lady's eye by the twinkling of his cross-gartered yellow stockings, Malvolio then as now stole the show: John Manningham went home with the ghost of the audience's laughter still in his ears, to jot down in his Diary for 2 February 1602 the first surviving contemporary allusion to *Twelfth Night*. What caught Manningham's imagination was the plot-device (he twice refers to a 'practise'), that imaginative egg laid by Maria's fertile wit and coddled and hatched by the conspirators, whereby Olivia's sober-sided steward is manipulated into exhibiting his day-dreams to the cruel light of public scorn. They can 'practise' upon Malvolio because they know exactly what he wants; he in turn 'practises' upon Olivia, in the attempt to give her what he thinks she wants, in return for what (the more he thinks about it) he's sure he wants – and can have. Malvolio packed the theatres, as Leonard Digges attested in commendatory verses published in 1640, for whereas the erudite productions of Ben Jonson might not cover production costs 'The Cockpit Galleries, Boxes, all are full / To heare *Malvoglio* that crosse garter'd Gull' (in Palmer, p. 25). Whereas some later generations came to think of *Twelfth Night* as the Play of Viola – spellbound by the gentle lyricism which surrounds the gallant, wistful figure at the play's romance heart – Renaissance audiences seem to have applauded the Play of Malvolio.

Manningham spotted nearly every major source, except perhaps Shakespeare's own early comedy, *The Two Gentlemen of Verona*, in which the themes of proxy-wooing by the disguised page-girl, the volatile and protean male lover, and the intensity of male friendship prefigure both matter and manner of the later comedy. Plautus's *Menaechmi* and Shakespeare's Plautine *The Comedy of Errors* provided models of plots in which a vertiginous maze of mistaken identities is based on the central motif of identical twins (though in both earlier plays these are male rather than male and female pairs). The Italian play, *Gl'Ingannati* (*The Deceived*) was written seventy years previously: Manningham notices this as a source, but not that it was probably passed on to Shakespeare more directly through Barnaby Rich's prose romance, 'Of Apolonius and Silla' in *Farewell to Military Profession* (1581), which features boy and girl siblings, of whom the sister, wrecked at sea and having escaped the lewd overtures of a libidinous Captain (quite unlike Shakespeare's civilized and obliging mariner), goes on to serve her beloved in the disguise of a page, calling herself by her brother's name Silvio. Silla's proxy-wooing of her beloved's beloved, Julina, prefigures Viola's of Olivia: 'Silvio, it is enough that you have said for your master. From henceforth either speak for yourself, or say nothing at all.' (Spencer, T. J. B. (ed.), *Elizabethan Love Stories*, p. 105). The real Silvio's arrival at Constantinople results in an amorous night with Julina, and her subsequent pregnancy. Silla, imprisoned by the Duke and named as the father of the child, is threatened with death unless she repairs Julina's honour by marrying her. Silla now demonstrates to Julina that 'he' *cannot*, by any stretch of the imagination, be the father:

And herewithal loosing his garments down to his stomach, and showed *Julina* his breasts and pretty teats, surmounting far the whiteness of snow itself, saying: 'Lo, madame, behold here the party whom you have challenged to be the father of your child. See, I am a woman, the daughter of a noble Duke . . .

(p. 115)

After this shock to everybody's system, the double marriage of the Duke to Silla and Julina to Silvio concludes the narrative.

Shakespeare concentrated, simplified and purged of explicit sexual adventure this central romance story. Breast-baring is out of the question not only for reasons of modesty but also because a boy-actor has none to bare – a pregnant fact which has an important, though ambivalent, bearing on how we respond to the play's sexuality. Viola is in a line of cross-dressing heroines from Julia in *Two Gentlemen*, Jessica and Portia in *The Merchant of Venice*, Rosalind in *As You Like It* and (later) Imogen in *Cymbeline*. The complexities of this androgynous figure will be considered later: here let me only note Shakespeare's indebtedness to the Spenserian Neoplatonist ideal of androgynous wholeness personified in the warrior-maidens of *The Faerie Queene*, especially Britomart, the fictional ancestor of Queen Elizabeth whose personal cult of quasi-divine female power they reinforce. From Greek and Roman myth, via Italian romance-epic (Boiardo, Ariosto, Tasso), Spenser inherited the figure of the 'martial maid' sacred to the warrior-goddess Diana, in whom qualities conventionally constructed as opposites in 'masculine' and 'feminine' are reconciled: vulnerable gentleness and heroic power, love and war, chaste beauty and valorous activity. In Spenser, these figures are uniquely lovable: they transcend the field of allegory to rise from the page as complex personalities. As questors who destabilize the patriarchal knightly norms, which, by appropriating, they transgress, they exert mysterious force which links them to the green world of Nature's powers and to the wholeness of Mother Nature herself, personified by Venus at her Temple in Book IV:

> they say, she hath both kinds in one,
> Both male and female, both under one name:
> She sire and mother is herself alone,
> Begets and eke conceives, ne needeth other none.
>
> (IV.x.41)

The hermaphrodite, a liminal figure etymologically compounded of Hermes plus Aphrodite, whose namesake Hermaphroditus so loved his mate Salmacis that they blissfully dissolved into one body, can be seen as either a freak or a miracle. In Spenser s/he bears the signature of the divine. Shakespeare's girl-pages are at once more homoerotically alluring and less subversive. They tend to faint at blood-curdling moments, their underlying girlishness transparent to the audience, their male disguise at once liberating and constraining. Viola is the martial maid comically bereft of martial capacities: the comedy of her mounting alarm in Act III at the thought of fighting the equally jittery and pusillanimous Sir Andrew plays upon what she 'lacks of a man'. Announced to her petrified antagonist as a 'firago' (ironically quibbling upon *virago*, female warrior) Viola/'Cesario' quakes in her shoes and expresses an urgent desire to run and hide up Olivia's skirts: 'I will return again into the house and desire some conduct of the lady. I am no fighter' (III.4.236–7). Nevertheless, something of the liminal Spenserian magic and the sense of human wholeness is vested in the ambivalent figure of the Shakespearian girl–boy: a sense of spiritual abundance and a startling eloquence, the keen and fencing word substituting for the sword. The 'female page' tradition was also a familiar motif in Elizabethan prose-romance (Montemayor's *Diana*, Lodge's *Rosalynde*, Sidney's *Arcadia*) and in romantic drama, the nearest to *Twelfth Night* being Lyly's delicately ironical *Gallathea*, whose two heroines, Phyllida and Gallathea, both disguised as boys, meet and fall in love with one another. In a scene prefiguring the 'Patience on a monument' scene between Orsino and Viola/'Cesario', Lyly's two girl–boys stroke each other with obliquely querying antennae, each fearing that the other might be a mirror-image of her own disguise:

PHYLLIDA	*Have you ever a sister?*
GALLATHEA	*If I had but one, my brother must needs have two. But, I*
	pray, have you ever a brother?
PHYLLIDA	*My father had but one daughter, and therefore I could*
	have no sister.

(III.2.35–9)

Viola's 'My father had a daughter loved a man –' (II.4.106) is a breathing echo of this dialogue, but the Shakespearian lyricism transmutes Lyly's dramatization of hoodwinking artifice as the subject of its own art (a play about representation by boy-actors) to this and something immeasurably deeper – an elegy for loss of self and kin which tells in fictional form an all-but-incommunicable truth.

Shakespeare grafted on to this Plautine and romance story two other actions: the 'festive' deception of Malvolio and the love-story of Antonio for Sebastian, a relationship which bears disturbing likeness to that expressed by the protagonist of Shakespeare's Sonnets for the fugitive 'master-mistress of my passion' (20). Any account of the scenic form of the play is therefore a discussion of the structural interweaving of these diverse materials, with their complex mirrorings and problematic disparities, as well as the contrapuntal styles which accompany them, from mellifluous lyricism to frantic intensity, teemingly imagistic prose with obsessive word-play and *basso profundo* cavortings in the lower reaches of Olivia's house. *Twelfth Night* is an entertainment which offers its audience gourmandizing variety, and indulges a hedonistic appetite not only for the ultra-refined pleasures suited to the sophisticated aesthete's palate of Orsino but also the party-enjoyments appropriate to the feast of Epiphany, when the whole household has been celebrating for at least a fortnight and ends with one almighty fling – a feast that turns rather sour in its latter stages, for some of the revellers at any rate. One major source for *Twelfth Night*, as C. L. Barber brilliantly showed, is the structure of Elizabethan holiday, with its saturnalian customs and its festive Lord of Misrule, a role represented in *Twelfth Night* by Sir Toby and Feste between them.

Stagecraft is paramount. Shakespeare's primary aim is to catch and keep the attention of the audience by variety of stimulations: altering pace; building expectation; prolonging suspense by failing to gratify expectation; alternating quiet and static scenes with only a few or a couple of characters with busy scenes of coming and going; building up tension and tempo as the play unfolds from the leisurely pace and conversational chattiness of the earlier Acts to the whirling farce with staccato surprises and release of violent emotion in the last two Acts. Principally the stage is a *locus*, the autonomous space where we view an imaginary world of characters which does not recognize our presence; alternatively, in soliloquy, it becomes a *platea* in which persons (recurrently Viola, but also Olivia, Antonio and Sebastian) turn away from that action to address us, the silent over-hearers, by confiding inner thoughts otherwise unspoken. Because of the privileged omniscience conferred on the audience by its witnessing in Act I, scene 2, of Viola's arrival at Illyria and her gender-disguise and in Act II, scene 1, of Sebastian's survival, together with Viola's frequent imparting of her deepest hopes, fears and perplexities in soliloquy proper and soliloquistic utterances whose full meaning is a secret to all but ourselves, the play is peculiarly rich in dramatic irony. Twice our omniscience is mimed by the existence of an internal audience on-stage, in set piece play-within-a-play scenes of virtuoso theatrical power: firstly, Malvolio's acting out of his fantasy-life and perusal of the forged letter in Act II, scene 4, with the seething 'audience' concealed in the box-tree (a text which he later uses as an acting-script in the 'yellow-stocking' scene (III.4)); secondly, the persecution of Malvolio in Act IV, scene 2, the climax of this plot, in which the conspirators again function as an internal audience. The audience's laughing collusion with this inner audience can be unsettling, calling attention, in some productions, to the sublimated violence implicit in the comic-experience. Yesterday we went to the bear-baiting at the Globe; today we are here to laugh at the Malvolio-baiting. The play-within-a-play device reinforces the self-reflexive thoughtfulness of a play which is always concerned with the potentially embarrassing nature and effects of play-acting, role-play, playing practical jokes, living according to a script, dressing up, and getting out of, or beyond, yourself.

Act I

The first Act is dedicated to the work of exposition, establishing a mood (and, as things develop, a variety of moods) and 'bonding' the audience, engaging its interest in the persons of the play and manipulating its sympathies, prejudices and desires, to be reinforced or undercut later. The opening lines of the play – crucial in projecting the theatrical illusion so as to engross the attention of the quietened audience – are among the most hypnotically memorable and quotable in Shakespearian drama:

> ORSINO *If music be the food of love, play on,*
> *Give me excess of it, that, surfeiting,*
> *The appetite may sicken, and so die.*
> *That strain again! It had a dying fall.*
> *O, it came o'er my ear like the sweet sound*
> *That breathes upon a bank of violets,*
> *Stealing and giving odour. Enough, no more!*
> *'Tis not so sweet now as it was before.*
>
> (I.1.1–8)

The musicality of this speech, together with its accompaniment to music, are discussed in detail later (see pp. 37–40 below). Tempo is leisurely, and while the speech takes its time to unfold, including a pause for the musical cadence to be repeated, the audience has a chance to dwell on the central languorous image of the aristocratic patron of the arts, speaking characteristically in the imperative (*play on*, *give me*, *again*, *Enough*), wordy, moody and lassitudinous, probably in a reclining posture emblematically appropriate to the love-sick 'amorist' whose role Orsino plays – a role balanced by Olivia's playing of the role of reclusive melancholic, introduced by Valentine in the second half of the scene (25–33). The enchantment of this speech is so soporifically mesmerizing that people who quote it do not always understand it: in essence, the whole speech is a very elegant way of saying that love, which feeds on beauty, devalues it; love's stomach binges on music, too much of which makes desire sick. This honey-tongued Duke, if we pause to think about it (which we possibly don't), is a very strange fish indeed. Direction of *Twelfth Night* needs superior finesse to make the instant ambiguities of the play apparent to the audience: the shot-silk, mercurial medium in which all Illyria's characters wander from colour into colour, mood to mood, illusion to illusion. The Duke's obsession with his stomach, a sort of digestive ocean, is only one of the grotesqueries which this play will dissolve in winy lyricism; just as the characters are bathed in Narcissus-like illusion, so we are washed over by the beautiful delusions of a strategically sophisticated verse. By virtue of our implication in this seducing music, we become for the three hours' duration courtesy Illyrians, drugged by the spoken word. *Enough, no more! / 'Tis not so sweet now as it was before*: as in so many mature Shakespearian plays, the whole is in the part and the part in the whole. *What you will* becomes, imperceptibly, too much – desire turns sour, the joke curdles, the feast begets a bilious morning-after feeling. The speech is proleptic of the total structure of *Twelfth Night*, its plotting of the arc of indulgence past limitation to excess, whereby sweet temper turns to gall – as witness Sir Toby's jaded 'I would we were well rid of this knavery' (IV.2.66–7) and his last, beastly dismissal of Sir Andrew: 'Will you help? An ass-head, and a coxcomb, and a knave, a thin-faced knave, a gull?' (V.1.203–4), to which Sir Andrew replies with appalled silence. Witness too the rude rages in the final Act: Antonio to Viola/'Cesario' ('a twenty years' removèd thing' (V.1.87)); Orsino to Olivia and her 'minion' (115–29); Sir Andrew to Viola/'Cesario' (181–91); and, topping them all, Malvolio in his famous *Exit* (375); and the odd-man-out Antonio's final, expressive silence, take it how you will.

From the tableau of the solitary Orsino talking preciously to his retainers about love-lorn reclusiveness, and complemented by the verbal picture of the unattainable beloved, the scene changes to another tableau, of Viola and the sea-captain, succinctly outlining her beached predicament, reinforcing the theme of brother-loss and moving with slick dexterity to the adoption of male disguise ('Conceal me what I am . . . Thou shalt present me as an eunuch to him' [I.2.54; 57]). Motives are confidently fudged by the playwright, in the expectation that the audience will not pause to ask questions; and, puzzlingly, Viola never does appear as advertised, whether a 'eunuch' or a musician, an inconsistency which has led critics to ascribe this detail to an uncorrected first draft. This important scene condenses much expository material and, just as crucially, begins the work of bonding Viola and the audience. It is one of the more curious of the illusions fathered on us by this beguiling play that we credit Viola's assumption of male disguise with a comprehensible rationale and her character with unimpeachable openness and consistency. Just as *Twelfth Night*'s characters savour putting one over on one another and are led by the nose through a world of illusion, so we, the audience, happily accept without a qualm that a person who points out with one breath that 'nature with a beauteous wall / Doth oft close in pollution' (49–50) should with the next breath suggest the adoption of a misleading disguise. It is partly, of course, that we are ready to accept the comic convention, but also that Shakespeare puts out for the audience the same trip-rope which the play's characters are to fall over – we too are to fall in love with Viola, more or less at first sight. Thus endeared, beguiled and yoked in solidarity with the play's love-object, we shall be willing to swallow any trickery as allowable *trompe-l'oeil*. Fresh from the sea, like Eros the child of Venus who arises from the sea in classical myth new-made with every morning, the ambisexual Viola will be all things to all men and women, including ourselves. Despite the Victorian congratulations earned by this play for its freedom from obscenity and bawdry, *Twelfth Night* is, in the seeing – and seeing is tasting and gratification – one of the more erotic plays of the period. In scene 2, the quality of sexual enchantment is not yet established (that is put on with the male disguise, which eroticizes the character). Instead, Viola's poetic voice is established, with its winning directness and simplicity, a compound of reticence and candour, sadness and hope, maturity and youthfulness. Like all natural speaking voices it has a unique but fugitive inflection, not devoid of metaphor but characteristically concise and free of excess ornament, founded on a simple grammar of direct statement. Whereas in the memorable scene with Olivia, we shall hear her expand into a witty poetry of great imaginative exuberance (I.5), this copious and lively rhetoric is always exerted in the defence of the plain, artless truth ('I see you what you are, you are too proud . . .', 'In your denial I would find no sense; / I would not understand it' (239; 255–6) – simple lexis, plain statement of reality). That is to say, her rhetorical elaborations reinforce the values of her own speaking voice. And, with a consonant irony, her tendency to riddle ('What I am and what I would are as secret as maidenhead' (207–8)) strikes the listener as a defence of her virgin integrity – a secrecy which, since it has been confided to the sympathetic audience, is never felt as duplicitous. Thus the theatrical illusion hoodwinks us into acceptance of the artless sincerity of this shape-changer who is playing havoc with Illyrian emotions. With the Duke, her speeches are short and subdued: her restraint in his presence impresses us with the ache of her listening presence, the fullness of the emotion that is withheld in the not-said. Act I, scene 2, has to lay down the characteristic manner of Viola's verbal music so that the audience can attune its ear to its cadences.

Olivia's household is entered, as it were, by the back entrance in the third scene, introducing the cacophonous feasters roistering in the nether regions at that sorrowing Lady's expense. The change of modulation, from the polished manners of the verse-speakers to the relaxed, wise-cracking prose of Sir Toby, is a recurrent tactic of the play, varying scenes between soft-spoken and loud-mouthed, cultivatedly witty and magnificently incontinent. Scene 3 moves into the anarchic realm of the festive spirit, where over-eating, boozing, staying up all night and reversing social and linguistic decorums are the unwritten law – a law which punishes infringers with the comic equivalent of public flaying. Dialogue between Maria and Sir Toby, with its rebuke of knight by servant ('By my troth, Sir Toby, you must come in earlier o'nights . . .' (3–4), and its defence of licence (9–12) by the bibulous knight, prefigures the central conflict between ethical order and comic disorder, and heralds the arrival of the vapid Sir Andrew, who is discussed for thirty lines before the audience is allowed to see him. The comic double act of Sir Toby and Sir Andrew (straight man and fall-guy) is a parodic variation on the musical theme, for Sir Toby's advertisement ('He plays o'the viol-de-gamboys' (23–4)) is belied by Sir Andrew's entire absence of cultivation and indeed of brain-cells, his amiable innocence of any culture including a merely nodding acquaintance with his native tongue. This scene sets up a rhetoric of comic hyperbole which establishes the play as an imaginative *tour de force* whose dynamic is the potential of language itself to conjure revelrous alternative worlds into momentary vision. Sir Toby's wit annihilates and re-creates Sir Andrew as a fantastic show-piece, a little nobody transformed by the afflatus of metaphor into all manner of inspirational shapes and purposes, from his hair (92–9) to his leg (124–33). Sir Andrew's whole life is translated into a performance-art in which he shines as genius and nonpareil. His simpleton's vanity at his dancing abilities ('And I think I have the back-trick, simply as strong as any man in Illyria' (116–17) not only evokes an easy laugh for the unconsciously bawdy suggestion but is picked up and turned into a stupendous vision of a life lived in a fantasy of dance:

Wherefore are these things hid? Wherefore have these gifts a curtain before 'em? Are they like to take dust, like Mistress Mall's picture? Why dost thou not go to church in a galliard and come home in a coranto? My very walk should be a jig. I would not so much as make water but in a sink-apace. What dost thou mean? Is it a world to hide virtues in? I did think by the excellent constitution of thy leg it was formed under the star of a galliard.

(118–26)

Accompanied no doubt by exemplary feints at agile leaps, dextrous bowings and arm-gestures, Sir Toby's linguistic and image-engendering versatility pumps up his victim's slow and bony little being, conspicuous for nothing at all, into a vast imaginative inflation which, the more its unlimited exploits are specified, the more comic glory accrues to the wordmonger manufacturing this phantom and the more absurdly small Sir Andrew remains. To piss as his legs sustain the intricate five-step cinquepace would be genius indeed – a humbly private function turned to a public glory of enactment. Sir Toby's essentially childish and exploitative humour is organized according to the rules of rhetoric, by balancing figures of speech and duplicating grammatical structures. The 'festive' energy in this lower plot is not raw and primitive, but served well-cooked and sauced: the dish of wit, in a play obsessively concerned with culture rather than nature, is the product of a gentleman's education. The function of this bravura exhibition of Sir Andrew is to arouse in the audience sheer joy in absurdity – to make us want more, and then more. The audience would also be made aware of Sir Andrew's legs – bean-poles, no doubt, spindle-shanks. Nothing perturbed, for he is innocently impervious to rebuff, from the subtlest to the grossest insult, Sir Andrew takes the compliment to his legs quite seriously: 'Ay, 'tis strong, and it does indifferent well in a dun-coloured stock' (127–8). No doubt he looks down with some complacency at the object of common admiration. By the end of the scene, Sir Toby has got him cutting a caper, an apt crescendo to the initiating scene, and proleptic too, for Sir Andrew's legs foreshadow Malvolio's legs – a man not given to dancing but who has something of Sir Andrew's susceptibility to anatomical flattery about him, unacknowledged even to himself, which Sir Toby will in turn fetch out and put on open exhibition, for 'Wherefore are these things hid?'

The short transitional scene 4 establishes Viola in her boy-disguise as the Duke's bosom-confidant, focusing on the ambivalence of her sexual appeal as a Narcissus-, Hermes- or Eros-figure, analogous to the 'lovely boy' of Shakespeare's Sonnets but showing an ironic and teasing image of her feminine self inside the male costume ('Diana's lip . . . Thy small pipe / . . . as the maiden's organ' (31–3)). On the Elizabethan stage, the transvestism is complicated by the ulterior transvestism of the boy-actor playing a girl playing a boy – erotically nearer to a pederastic dream than modern convention allows (see pp. 113 ff.). The scene is dominated by the Duke's giving of orders (nine verbs in the imperative mood, all the rest declaratory or predictive), sending Viola to woo her own rival, as we gather in the soliloquistic couplet which ends the scene (41–2). The scene is more important dramatically than its length on the page implies: it must focus the unusual intimacy, amounting to fascination which the Duke feels for Viola/'Cesario', together with his *identification* with the boy – a man with no secure sense of a self sending out an image or self-projection to 'act my woes' (26). The girl–boy sidles into an ambiguous synthesis of roles: she both mirrors Orsino as subject and is (obscurely and obliquely) loved as object. Viola's surrogacy is at the centre of her healing role in the Duke's and also Olivia's rootbound lives: as a hermetic messenger she runs between them like a moving mirror on which each reads his or her own face, autonomously free, challenging them to move and capture it. Like narcissi reflecting upon themselves in a still pool, they would otherwise have remained in barren stasis. As messenger, Viola mimes the role of the Greek double-gendered Hermes, able to divert their downward-gazing eyes and impel them into the world of action.

The final scene of Act I, where the Fool, Olivia and Malvolio enter for the first time, establishes the atmosphere of misrule and conflict at Olivia's house; it mills with people (Sir Toby coming in drunk, retainers squabbling, a visitor announced first by Maria, then Sir Toby, then by Malvolio going off and returning with information). The play presents for the first time an impression of a complex community, hierarchical but discordant and combustible: the antagonistic poles of the household, Feste and Malvolio, confront one another for the first time here, and Malvolio's contumely towards the Fool gives the offence for which he will have to pay in the course of the play ((70–84); quoted nearly verbatim by the Fool in the last Act (V.1.372–3)). The scenic form depends on accumulation of dramatic expectation, with the series of announcements of the Duke's 'gentleman's' arrival at the gate (Maria, (94–5); Sir Toby, (113); a long narrative with reported speech by Malvolio, (134–56)), until curiosity is gratified in a carefully structured scene of meeting between Viola and Olivia, which gives visual form to *Twelfth Night*'s preoccupation with problems of identity by the veiling (159–60) and mock-ceremonious unveiling of Olivia's face, with its suggestion of veils beneath veils as the reality revealed is suspected as a representation: 'we will draw the curtain and show you the picture' (223). The nude face can be a front, a mask or a bare-faced lie – 'Excellently done – if God did all' (226). But the moment of revelation can be mysteriously thrilling on the stage, recalling Orsino's allusion to Actaeon's viewing of the nude Diana in the first scene (see pp. 51–2). Symbolically, at this moment, Olivia comes out of hiding, and opens herself to the destabilizing threats of love. The exchange moves through a richly nuanced dialogue of mutual curiosity, banter, blarney and the burst of lyric poetry in the famous 'willow cabin' speech which marks the crucial turning-point in Olivia's emotions: 'You might do much. / What is your parentage?' (266), which, with comic authenticity, gets briskly down to basics before risking all (is this young man eligible?). This fall into love is charted as a subtle process: the whole scene gradually builds up and plays on an intense fascination in the characters for one another. It exemplifies one of the most extraordinary features of the play's

11

poetic manner: the implication of the unsaid. Reticences and indirections have a speaking poignancy, so that we intuit the conflict Viola feels when she sees how beautiful her rival really is, as she removes her veil, speaking through the ironic veil of her own disguise (228 ff.); we have inklings of Olivia's arousal as her attention begins to centre on the hypnotic messenger rather than his message ('What are you? What would you?' (204–5)). The sleeper is awoken by a benignly intending mischief-maker, carried away by her part and unable to check until too late the vitality which she brings to it. It is in this important scene that the first great erotic delusion in *Twelfth Night* is lingeringly engendered, and the play begins to reflect upon its own means of representation as a subject in its own right. The medium of acting, and people as actors in manufactured or unconscious roles, become the subjects under scrutiny as Olivia enters the tricky realm of illusion and self-delusion, smitten by blind Eros in the person of the 'lovely boy'. Her two bitter-sweet soliloquies (278–87; 298–301) complete the playwright's exposition of Illyria, so that the whole range of its notes from treble to bass have been sounded (with the exception of the comic straight-man, Fabian, who is introduced only in Act II, scene 5, to swell out the group of conspirators to a fivesome).

Act II

Shakespeare has reserved one piece of expository material until the second Act: the adroit delay in producing Antonio and Sebastian in 'another state further along the coast of the Adriatic' has had the effect of isolating Viola with her uncertainty over her twin's survival, as a lonely outsider far from kin and home. Having established the bond of sympathy between audience and Viola, the playwright now feeds in the second twin, as a promise of final comic fulfilment, while simultaneously arousing the elegiac sense of mystery surrounding their family-loss by imagery of death by drowning: 'My father . . . a sister, both born in an hour . . . some hour before you took me from the breach of the sea was my sister drowned', 'She is drowned already, sir, with salt water', 'I am yet so near the manners of my mother' (II.1.15, 17, 19–20; 26–7; 35–6). The repetitions are incantatory. Family dissolution, a life reborn without bearings after shipwreck – 'father . . . sister . . . sister . . . mother' – echoes the lyric note of wistful longing established by Viola in the play's second scene. Or rather, Sebastian (himself a double-named twin and a shape-changer – 'my name is Sebastian, which I called Roderigo' (14–15)) sounds the echo of an echo, for *Twelfth Night* is so profoundly

12

restrained in its emotional inflections that when the play sounds this theme of homesickness its very understatement creates a peculiarly remote and haunting quality, like shoreline music heard in the distance. Antonio's passion for Sebastian adds another dimension to the same-sex relationships already established, so that where in the previous scene wc have viewed the girl-twin loved by a woman, here we enjoy its corollary, the boy-twin loved by a man. Dramatic symmetries, parallels and contrasts are so disposed as to present diptych or mirroring effects between scenes as the playwright shifts the scene from one image to its opposing reflection. The theme of narcissism, together with the narrative of Narcissus and Echo (see p. 59 below) are thus built visually into the arrangement of the action, as one scene opposes predecessor and successor in mirror-reversal. This scene, the only one to be set outside Illyria, is also crucial in giving the audience priority of information over Viola: heretofore, insight has been even, but now we are privileged to hold the one piece of information she would give the world to have. Hence, the dizzy distress of her cross-wooing conundrum expressed in her soliloquy in the following scene, having received the ring from Malvolio (II.2.17–41), can be fully savoured by the audience as a comic 'knot', in the security that her brother has just popped up and is getting closer.

Act II is dominated by the two mighty episodes which determine Malvolio's ignominious topple from his high horse (scenes 3 and 5), interrupted for the purposes of contrast by the 'Patience on a monument' scene between Orsino and his 'boy'. This structure of contrasts between the noise of revelrous high spirits and the quiet of mutual reverie is dramatically very powerful. Scene 3 rings with boozy, bawdy stage-action and singing, the explosion of Malvolio on to the scene; the row; his huffy egress and the punitive intrigue of the plotters. Scene 4 between Orsino and Viola suspends the fulfilment of this design by returning us to the cultured interior of Orsino's house, where soft-spoken tongues communicate in silken poetry and music suffuses the entire scene. Tempo, which has already been slowed at the end of scene 3 as the late-night party dies on its feet in slurred and maudlin reminiscence and yawning fatigue as Sir Andrew drops his pearl 'I was adored once, too' (174), slows down further with the elevation to blank verse and the hush that surrounds Feste's song 'Come away death'. The action takes on the regularity of slow breathing with many pauses and spell-binding passages of thought, as Viola almost gives herself away, confiding herself through riddling fictional projections of her situation and feelings. The emotion of the scene is at once intense and subtle, as she captures, then rivets, Orsino's attention, enclosing the two of them in the breathing intimacy of private space. At the end of this mesmerizingly beautiful exchange, the tempo switches abruptly, as Viola snaps alert: 'Sir, shall I to this lady?' (121), and contemplation gives way to action. Again, maximum contrast is achieved in the next scene (5) which rudely exposes Malvolio basking in pleasurable soliloquy, his overheard fantasy punctuated by the secret fellows in the box-tree, the violent expostulations of Sir Toby having to be squelched by Fabian ('Out, scab!' / 'Nay, patience, or we break the sinews of our plot' (74–5)). The scene is composed of repeated rhythms of interruptions and interruptions of interruptions, retarding with quick-fire interjection the onward motion of Malvolio's magnificently comic fantasy, so that he seems perpetually suspended in mid-sentence. This repetition sets up a ritual pattern of expectancy in the audience. When Malvolio picks up the bait of the forged letter, action becomes exhaustively self-retarding. Every word, every letter of the counterfeit has to be gone through and evaluated in Malvolio's gormless Latinity: 'But then there is no consonancy in the sequel; that suffers under probation: "A" should follow, but "O" does' (127–8). The conspirators constantly stress his snail's pace cracking of a riddle which is child's play, forcing the audience's attention to centre on the irritating pace of what is happening, or just failing to happen – a mind crawling forward on a short journey of miraculous longevity. The climax of the scene comes as Malvolio bursts out of this painstaking labour into triumphant self-acclamation: 'This is open. I will be proud, I will read politic authors, I will . . .' (154–5). He is being reborn before our eyes as Count-Malvolio-To-Be, a fantasy-figure delivered from prodigious travail and swollen to gargantuan inflation. The audience greets the phantasm with wild jubilation. Malvolio's deluded state at the climax of Act II now mimes Olivia's at the end of Act I: more headily intoxicated than the play's actual drunkards, they stand in a state of precarious exaltation, enrolled with the fools and braying asses. It remains for Shakespeare to bring the incompatible madnesses together.

However, the structure of Act II is not merely a matter of dynamic contrast: the life of the play flows through from scene to scene with a pleasing fluency, so that (for instance) both scenes 3 and 4 share the music provided by the Clown, whose songs in both scenes distil a comparable emotion. 'O mistress mine!' (3.37–50) and 'Come away, come away, death' (4.50–65) were evidently composed by Shakespeare to exploit the singing voice of the actor in his company (Robert Armin) who took the Clown's role. A reader can never reproduce in her mind's ear the atmospheric difference imparted by the movement from spoken to sung language: time is lulled as action is suspended, and a raptness falls on stage and auditorium as Feste's art harmonizes love-pangs which, for the duration, no longer gripe and humiliate but calm and delight. *Twelfth Night* favours, as does Tudor and early Stuart music as a whole, the music with a 'dying fall' commended by Orsino in the first scene (see pp. 38–9 below). The play takes on – transiently and ironically in scene 3 but expansively in scene 4 – the quality of madrigal or ayre, the popular music of the day. In a play subtitled *What You Will*, musical diversion is considered an essential ingredient of pleasure. Sir Toby will pay sixpence for it, cash in hand, and Sir Andrew comes up with the same amount (3.30–33). The song itself obscurely concentrates the essence of the play: the fugitive 'mistress' (Olivia), the arrival of the ambiguous musician-lover (Viola) who can sing both treble and baritone, the call to present enjoyment. This song is succeeded by the singing of vernacular canon catches and ballads, culminating in the ironic rendition of 'Farewell, dear heart', suitably adapted to outrage the ears of the impotent Malvolio (3.99–109), immediately before the powerful centre of the scene in the famous 'cakes and ale' defence of comedy against the custodians of decorum and repression. Thus music is made a discourse of the play: Sir Toby not only speaks against Malvolio but sings against him, bombarding his affronted eardrums with uncontrollable love of pleasure.

In the next scene (4) the Duke recapitulates the first entrance he made in the play by autocratically demanding another dose of his addictive anodyne: 'Give me some music!' and music is played and discussed through the first half of the scene, building up desire for and expectation of another song. Feste is not there and has to be sent for. Orsino therefore orders some background music to be played as an intermezzo, both gratifying hunger for the 'food of love' and delaying the gratification. 'How dost thou like this tune?' he asks the 'boy': 'It gives a very echo to the seat / Where love is throned' (4.20–22). Viola's use of the word *echo* echoes the echo-effect of her 'willow cabin' speech (I.5.257–65): like Narcissus pining after his own watery image and Echo pining after the pining Narcissus, the two figures present an arresting tableau, each speaking out of an almost tangible isolation in an ironic recitative which, by oblique steps, brings them wandering into a private closeness in which only the shadow of a veil seems to separate them – and yet they remain separate. The method of progressive self-concealing self-revelation by which Shakespeare develops this process makes the scene at once nervously tense and profoundly touching. Communication from Viola to the Duke has to be shown proceeding on an all but subliminal level, a waking dream-speech as if the antennae of the Duke's subconscious mind were alerted by the tiniest of signals to the nearness of his ultimate counterpart. Upon the success of this scene's negotiation of a transition in his emotions depends the credibility of his later transference from Olivia to Viola in Act 5. 'Thou dost speak masterly' he congratulates her, taken with her effortless eloquence and naturally inclined to attribute such power over language to his servant's male *mastery* of the tongue. His curiosity aroused, he interrogates the youth whose experience seems so far beyond his years:

> *My life upon't, young though thou art, thine eye*
> *Hath stayed upon some favour that it loves.*
> *Hath it not, boy?*
>
> VIOLA   *A little, by your favour.*
> ORSINO   *What kind of woman is't?*
> VIOLA   *Of your complexion.*
> ORSINO   *She is not worth thee, then. What years, i'faith?*
> VIOLA   *About your years, my lord.*
> ORSINO   *Too old, by heaven . . .*
>
>   (II.4.23–9)

Dramatic irony rests on the literal truthfulness of Viola's equivocating answers: she never tells a lie. She feigns, and through the veil of feigning shows the natural lineaments of truth quite nakedly – a truth which Orsino, being blinded, cannot see, though his growing alertness to some mysterious presence or present mystery shows like that of someone in a trance who feels he is tapped on the shoulder and turns to find nobody there, or hears his name called by a familiar voice in a crowd. This sense of uncanny proximity is suggested with colloquial naturalness. Through Viola's tentative, half playful, half rueful answers, subdued and opaquely direct, the artificial scene assumes an air of flowing ease: even in the reading, the simple give and take of short half-line exchanges seems to lift off the page with the idiomatic naturalness of the speaking voice. Viola tells all – while telling nothing – and as the Duke's perplexed objection to the idea of the lad being in love with a female clone of himself implies that he in turn understands nothing, the scene may also be played in such a way that he receives more than an inkling of 'Cesario's' devotion to himself. The truth of fiction is the scene's great theme. The play on relative ages has an ironic nuance. The *status quo* in the form of master and lad; man and woman; older and younger, holds the stage. But the stage revises and reverses the hierarchy in maintaining it: this boy is self-evidently maturer than his elder; this girl wiser than the man; the reticent servant says more than 'his' garrulous superior. As we move through the scene, the preponderance of the Duke's speaking role is overwhelming, up to the break in their colloquy marked by the song. Gender-relations and the melancholy imbalance between the sexes which tells against the female, arc the focus of all conversation, together with a profound sensitivity, typical of Shakespeare's writing, to the sufferings of women in a world where power is monopolized by the male, and where women are confined to a passive, wordless role, at the man's fickle mercy. Ironically, Viola's confinement in male disguise duplicates the common experience of suppression and muting:

> ORSINO   *For women are as roses whose fair flower,*
>   *Being once displayed, doth fall that very hour.*
> VIOLA   *And so they are. Alas, that they are so,*
>   *To die, even when they to perfection grow.*
>
>   (II.4.38–41)

This modulation from the flow of supple and idiomatic verse to the couplet in which the Duke sums up the patriarchal commonplace of the perishability of female beauty and hence her merely short-term value (a fall into abatement and low price) is dramatically a movement towards the music of Feste's song, for Viola's melancholy couplet, with its chiastic reversal – *so . . . are*: *are so* – on the first line, gives an echo and re-echo to the Duke's, like the choric plaint at the end of a song. Stylization works to dissolve pain in lyricism. And now Curio and the Clown enter: dramatic expectation is fulfilled as the idea of dying for love ('Come away, death') is set to music at the heart of the scene.

The second half of the scene echoes this theme in the major key. Relative roles are reversed as the Duke's monopolization of the main speaking voice is gradually ceded to Viola. Viola speaks, as it were, for Echo, in a voice that communicates a peculiar inwardness, midway between a soliloquist's reverie and an intensely expressive metaphorical delivery of an urgent message. The artful construction of the scene leads from Orsino's unexamined assumptions that his suit to Olivia *must* succeed, simply because it is his and he can't be said 'no' to (86–7), and that women are by nature fickle and inferior (92–102), through Viola's camouflaged telling of her own story ('Say that some lady, as perhaps there is . . .' (88)) and the rashly impulsive near give-away of the secret of her own disguise ('Ay, but I know . . .' (102)) to the autobiographical parable by which Viola fixes the Duke's fascination upon herself by begetting a fictional version of her own stifled feelings (109–120). There is nothing quite like the delicately nuanced beauty of this scene in Renaissance drama: we can pluck 'sources' out of Lyly's *Gallathea* and Shakespeare's own *The Comedy of Errors*, but such comparisons mirror a merely surface likeness. Viola's poetry and the Duke's rapt attentiveness (lifted for the first time quite out of himself and looking reality – that is, the disguised Viola – in the face) represent the most purely imaginative phase in a play which is dedicated to the 'high fantastical'. Sensitive productions of *Twelfth Night* take care to observe the moments of pause and silent self-communing, which sustain a dramatic rhythm composed of what can be said and what cannot be said, from the taking of breath before Viola begins her fable ('My father had a daughter loved a man –' (10)) to the two or possibly three pauses in the lines which end the sequence ('I am all the daughters of my father's house, / And all the brothers too; and yet, I know not . . . / Sir, shall I to this lady?' (119–21)). These pauses are meditation-spaces, the silences which cover that which cannot be said, an absence of words which signifies loss. Just as 'breathing' is all-important in the projection of voice as song, so in these most musical cadences, the actors have to attune their breathings to the timings and inflections of a duet which moves insistently towards solo. The recurrence of the father/daughter/ brother trinity enhances our sense of the solitude of Viola: she features herself as a relict, the left-over life of a dynasty and the sole survivor of trauma involving a severed bond with the past. Identityless as a mirror, like a face estranged from the person who wears it, she balances the identityless Orsino, a person equally lacking in kin and empty of certainty. The funerary symbolism of Viola's great elegy for a version of herself – the pining girl whose history was a 'blank' – picks up something of the frozen calm in which Viola survives the trauma of family-loss as well as the atrophy of hope behind a disguise that has begun to assume a sinister aspect.

> ORSINO   *And what's her history?*
> VIOLA   *A blank, my lord. She never told her love,*
>   *But let concealment, like a worm i'the bud,*
>   *Feed on her damask cheek. She pined in thought,*
>   *And with a green and yellow melancholy,*
>   *She sat like Patience on a monument,*
>   *Smiling at grief. Was this not love indeed?*
>   *We men may say more, swear more, but indeed*
>   *Our shows are more than will; for still we prove*
>   *Much in our vows, but little in our love.*
>   (II.4.108–17)

The grieving speechlessness of the imaginary girl, immobile as a statue, represents the constraint of passive silence with which society mutes women's expression of desire. Ironically, Viola's male disguise condemns her to a fictional version of this mute destiny. The fixed and sculpted smile on the girl's face is itself a disguise, resembling the marmoreal icon of 'Patience' outlasting the dead and all their untold stories. From the flowing polyphony of the play's music emerges a single, spell-binding voice like an ayre after a madrigal, telling of the threshold between living and dead, lover and beloved. Viola's musical language never more inspirationally echoes the suggestions of her name, the viol which (like the lute) would accompany the solo voice in ayres, its own speech eloquent though wordless – so eloquent indeed that voice and viol could 'sing' each other's parts in the score. The fluent melodic curves of Viola's impromptu conclude in a rhyming couplet whose internal rhyme *will:still* reinforces the graceful antithesis of *much:little* upon which the final dactyllic metre comes to rest.

The great theatrical power of this scene resides in its gradual suspension of time and cessation of action. The text's notation requires of the voice, which is now the centre of the drama, the subtlest and most exact of phrasing. Tempo slows almost to complete stillness. Then there is the contrast of renewed call to action: 'Sir, shall I to this lady?' (121). Stage business is resumed; the stage becomes a place of eddying action and noise, all the more dynamic because time has just been suspended. The audience rubs its eyes and stretches its legs as though roused from waking dream. We have indulged the pleasures proper to pathos while enjoying privileged knowledge of the survival of Viola's twin. Her musing 'and yet, I know not' is inwardly answered by our 'But we do – we've seen him': *Twelfth Night* is a feast of subtle and less subtle pleasures which permissively lets us have our cake and eat it. We censure the Duke for self-indulgence while indulging the fabricated sentiments of the play in their delicious fullness. We mock Olivia's deluded imagination while ourselves enjoying the glamorous doubleness of a crafty and artful Viola whom we agree to accept as God's own truth. Thus the play constantly refers us back to ponder the nature of the dramatic illusion. And yet it remains a mysterious paradox of *Twelfth Night* that during this scene the stage is more haunted by the shadowy presence of the lost brother (and the father with whom he shares a name) than in the scenes in which we view him in the flesh. Wherever Viola is, the boy-twin is also spectrally present for our eyes to see: she is his living mnemonic. In the timeless moments of Act II, scene 4, that uncanny doubling is at its most intense. The dead cannot fade while we remember and memorialize them – the stage is alive with resonances, mirrorings. Because we know that the twin brother has been preserved and is waiting in the wings to be delivered at the ripe time, the scene's melancholy can be savoured as serene beauty. And we are more than prepared to devote ourselves to the 'sport' of the Malvolio-baiting with the newly introduced Fabian (2.5) in that we have the pleasure of the lengthy prolongation of our expectation of the homing boy-twin's eventual return.

Act III

Act III imparts a more violent momentum to the play's action, though it begins with a leisurely dialogue between Viola and the Fool which reflects wittily on the language of folly (see pp. 82–3 below), culminating in Viola's soliloquy of tribute to fools (58–66). By the end of this Act, Olivia's infatuation with Viola will have reached frenzy-pitch; Sir Toby will have cooked up the second conspiracy, the duel between Sir Andrew and Viola (scene 2); Antonio, having landed at Illyria with Sebastian, will have handed over his purse to his friend (laying the groundwork for an imagined betrayal (scene 3). The lengthy, explosive and complex fourth scene produces on the stage every major character except the Duke and Feste. It has two climaxes, one at its beginning and one at its end, opening with Malvolio's immortal performance in the yellow stockings, cross-gartered and smiling, followed by his baiting by Fabian, Sir Toby and Maria, and the pumping-up of the duel between Sir Andrew and his 'rival' Viola (really Sir Toby's rival, for a successful suitor to his niece will mark the end of his misrule in her house). The second climax of the scene, Antonio's irruption, aborting the duel and mistaking Viola for Sebastian, sets whirling another violent spiral of bewilderment and anger: lyricism gives place to the rallentando scuffles of farce and the complications and virtuoso solutions of a plotting reminiscent of *The Comedy of Errors*. Given the probability that Elizabethan performances broke for an interval at the end of Act III, and that plays therefore tended towards division into two-part structures with a new beginning at Act IV, the poet of *Twelfth Night* had left himself with a great deal of stage-work to complete in Act III so as to arrive at a satisfactory pause. Some of the Act seems to consist of purely functional 'bridging' work, notably the somewhat forced scene between Sebastian and Antonio (3) in which some expository narrative explains why he is *persona non grata* in Illyria, and the purse is handed over. Such pressure on material would also explain the length and complexity of the final scene (4).

In Act III, Shakespeare rings tonal and rhythmic changes on material previously introduced: a kind of transitional passage towards the key-change in Act IV. Thus the mood of Act III is the last phase on the way to frenzy, from Olivia's desperate frustration to Malvolio's comparable 'midsummer madness' (4.56), Viola's bad state of nerves at the prospect of the duel, and Antonio's explosion (356 ff.). Frenetic humour characterizes the action, starting with the Olivia/Viola tussle of wills and wits in scene 1, whose increasing stylization is paradoxically a measure of emotional tumult, with the bravura display of quick-fire riddles, dominated by Viola, formalized as stichomythia, taken at a mad pace, like a reel of Laingian psychological knots:

> OLIVIA *Stay.*
> *I prithee, tell me what thou think'st of me?*
> VIOLA *That you do think you are not what you are.*
> OLIVIA *If I think so, I think the same of you.*
> VIOLA *Then think you right; I am not what I am.*
> OLIVIA *I would you were as I would have you be.*
> VIOLA *Would it be better, madam, than I am?*
> *I wish it might, for now I am your fool.*
>
> (I.134–41)

This round of verbal fencing is followed by the exchange of versified vow and counter-vow, ritually professing and disavowing love between persons totally at cross-purposes (146–61). Scene 2, in which Sir Toby and Fabian work Sir Andrew up to challenge his 'rival' suitor, is a feast of language in the form of perspectivist conceits, unique even in this teeming play (see pp. 86–7 below). Maria's late entrance in the scene (64) acts as a public advertisement of the comic riches to come in the Malvolio plot, but Sir Toby's conclusion of the scene, 'Come, bring us, bring us where he is' (80), with its eager repetition, is immediately balked by the strategic interposition of the Sebastian/Antonio scene. Yet another advertisement by Maria heralds the arrival of Malvolio ('Sweet Lady! Ho! Ho!' (4.17)) for his finest hour, not a syllable of whose conversation is comprehensible to Olivia. Once again his sentences (quotations from the forged letter) hang suspended, as his knowing recitation is rhythmically broken up by incredulous repetition and expostulation (38–55). His soliloquy (65–83) with its state of wild delusion is followed by the taunting by his persecutors, in which he enters an empyrean of indignity, a state of which he is sublimely unconscious. From this innocence he is about to fall precipitately into the angry knowledge that he has been put to shame, but this self-consciousness (never self-knowledge) is not reached until Act IV – after the interval – when all on the stage maddens and darkens, as Sir Toby predicts (134–140).

The join between this episode and the challenge which will take up the next two hundred lines is little more than a functional parataxis: 'More matter for a May morning!' (141) as the second intrigue gets under way, and Sir Andrew, entering and reading aloud the second letter in the play (there are three, in Acts II, III and V) inaugurates the martial encounter between cowards, each seeing the other magnified through false report into the essence of machismo. First Viola's terror is blown up like a great balloon by the fabrication of a ferocious reputation for Sir Andrew, by verbal sleight laced with authenticating detail ('a devil in a private brawl. Souls and bodies hath he divorced three;' (231–2)) and larded with dueller's slang ('Hob, nob! is his word: give't or take't' (235)). Then Sir Andrew is produced and given the same treatment ('a firago . . . They say he has been fencer to the Sophy' (268; 272)). Scenic structure thus depends on a rhythm of symmetrical repetitions, building up comic tension towards the reluctant but inevitable action of confrontation – a confrontation which never takes place. In place of the pleasure of expectation satisfied is substituted the greater pleasure of surprise, as the Antonio/Sebastian story suddenly bursts through to fuse with the Illyrian story at the very place where its two plots join. Ironically, Antonio is a war-hero whose exploits have a foreign maleness and attack. Sebastian is destined to dole out comic punishments to the intriguers in the form of thrashings. Antonio's mistaking of Viola for Sebastian, ushering in wave after wave of mis-identifications in the last two Acts, is the climax of the first half, the end of the beginning and the beginning of the end. But penultimately, the Act modulates into an exquisite 'dying fall', a brief return to the andante music of meditation, as Viola picks up from Antonio her brother's name:

> *Prove true, imagination, O, prove true –*
> *That I, dear brother, be now ta'en for you! . . .*
>
> *. . . I my brother know*
> *Yet living in my glass . . .*
>
> *O, if it prove,*
> *Tempests are kind, and salt waves fresh in love!*
> (4.366–7; 370–71; 374–5)

The haunting solo voice again sounds the mysterious key-note of the play, not so very far from Keats's 'truth of the imagination, and the holiness of the heart's affections'. Within the corporate illusion of the play, the imagination (as Viola begins to hope and we trust) and only the imagination has authentic reality: Viola's balanced cadences, somewhere between wish and prayer, express a desire with which the whole audience sympathetically collaborates. The artistry of the play is continuously to arouse and simultaneously to hold off gratification of this desire. Even when fulfilment comes, in Act V, the recognition-scene will be dispensed lingeringly, a slow, held-back process of gradual awakening, prolonging a pleasure which, delayed and savoured, is bounteous in proportion to its incompletion. Desire is the play's subject, not fulfilment, and *Twelfth Night* uses all conceivable means to head off the anticlimax of resolution (Viola never changes back into normal female clothes and therefore remains suspended in ambivalence as an object of desire; Malvolio shatters the complacency of the closure; the Clown lingers in the doorway and sings of the unsatisfactoriness of human life). Viola's 'kind tempests' and fresh salt waves speak of a benign Fortune which prefigures the Last Plays with their baptismal Providential sea-symbolism, but here the theme is all the more haunting for being muted, the sea heard as if in a shell, distantly evocative. However, these lyrical echoes are not the Act's last word: that belongs to Sir Toby's jaded cynicism, looking forward to the buffoonery of non-events to come. 'Come, let's see the event' says Fabian (385), looking forward to Sir Andrew's new eagerness to wallop 'Cesario' now that he is detected as a weakling. 'I dare lay any money, 'twill be nothing yet' comments Sir Toby, exiting (386): in the play's conflict between romantic and anti-romantic elements, earth-bound bathos has the last word in the first half.

Act IV

Act IV is a concise movement of three scenes. It announces an explosive turn as four Illyrians (Feste, Sir Andrew, Sir Toby and Olivia) mistake Sebastian for Viola in scene 1; scene 2 presents the culmination of the Malvolio plot in the black humour of the prison scene, the first of two comic climaxes in the play (the second being the reunion of the twins in Act V); scene 3, again centring on Sebastian, shows him forcibly haled off to solemn betrothal by Olivia in one of the rudest shot-gun wooings in literary history. In the parenthetically enclosing scenes 1 and 3, Shakespeare is hurrying on the major plot towards its climax in the final Act. The central scene of comic exorcism (discussed more fully on

23

pp. 107–12) has a uniquely turbulent resonance as it centres on the (to us) invisible voice of the imprisoned Malvolio tormented by the manic antics of the (to him) invisible voice of the alleged Sir Topas, a scene most accurately denoted by the phrase '*terribly* funny'. But the Act has an internal unity in its weaving of these three scenes into the unfolding of a design which oscillates between the harrowing and the vertiginous. The sequence presents an extreme of traumatized disorientation, the darkly orgiastic side of Illyria's comic ambiguities, sister-state to the Ephesus of *The Comedy of Errors* in which tailors you never met call you into their shops to measure you up for clothes you haven't ordered (IV.3.7–9); strange women ravingly claim you for a husband (II.2.119 ff.) and broils break out on incomprehensible grounds. The bewitched-seeming Illyria of Act IV is an identity-threatening whirlpool which seems set on disorientating Sebastian and Malvolio into dizziness on the one hand and craziness on the other. Each in his own way resists. Sebastian knocks hell out of his antagonist. The stage runs amok with unprecedented riot (1), giving the audience the primitive pleasure of pugilistic revenge, at least on Sir Andrew, though Sir Toby's is reserved for the final Act. The joke is already on the turn against its perpetrators: the chief engineer is no longer in full control, and skulks or stalks off-stage under Olivia's imperative, 'Rudesby, be gone!' (50). Viola is unprecedentedly an absentee, leaving the stage clear for her baffled brother. His 'Are all the people mad?' (26) gives the key-signature to the Act, linking it with the Ephesus of *The Comedy of Errors* – but with significant differences. Ephesus for the Syracusan twin has both a sanity-threatening and a seamy side, ripe with jaded ironies.

ANTIPHOLUS OF SYRACUSE   *The fellow is distract, and so am I,*
And here we wander in illusions.
Some blessed power deliver us from hence!
Enter a Courtesan

(IV.3.42–4)

'Fortune's a right whore', as Renaissance dramatists agreed (Webster, *The White Devil*, I.i.5) and as Shakespeare's cynical stage direction implies: but there are no courtesans discernible in Illyria whose climate (to the dazzled eye of Sebastian) has a radiance and freshness, communicated as he emerges in scene 3 – 'This is the air; that is the glorious sun' (1). Whereas the Syracusan twin was having a rough and nasty time in Ephesus, the boy-twin in Illyria feels himself to be in a state of crazy beatitude, swept off to be married to the unstoppable Lady at the end of the Act, with mild acquiescence. The tumultuous scene 1 concludes with a presage of troth-plighting in which Olivia and Sebastian reverse the hierarchical roles of bride and groom: to Olivia's inquiry as to whether he will 'be ruled by me!', Sebastian equably answers, 'Madam, I will' (63–4); hustled off to be sworn at the end of scene 3, they repeat this rhythm with a brief versified ritual (32–5). Then *Exeunt*, the playwright having tied a knot between the two plots which will ultimately salvage Olivia's happiness and in the interim breed a late flurry of complications (as Olivia wrestles with her imagined husband, 'Cesario').

The grace and benediction which the wild events of Act IV dole out to the boy-twin are not extended to Malvolio (unless you are one of those who believe that Malvolio's noble resistance to the preposterous catechism of his captor raises him into a state of grace). This scene, representing the second of the play-within-a-play devices, plots concentric circles around the sealed centre of attention: the boxed-up Malvolio, with the Fool running rings around him, watched by the malevolent Sir Toby, exerting himself without much success to suck the last juice out of the intrigue, overseen by our good selves – or our complicit selves, or (by this time) tense and neurotic, but probably still laughing, selves. Laughter, which generally siphons off tension, may here recharge it. Discomfort is a common response to this part of the play. Other witnesses, less queasy about practical jokes, regard the scene as the highest point of *Twelfth Night*'s hilarity, a licensed relieving of violent mirth-contractions (and after all, Malvolio, who had it coming, is not giving way to panic and will soon be free). Few scenes as richly exhibit not only the essential volatility and openness to interpretation of Shakespearian comedy, but also its dynamic theatrical power. The scene is self-advertisingly a show: it exhibits Malvolio as a caged freak and taunts him with his singularity. If the 'Patience on a monument' scene between Viola and Orsino (II.4.113) is the heart of the play, this scene is something like its backside. Here the intrigue goes bad, the joke sickens and can never be amended. Sir Toby's abdication from the abortive intrigue, strategically placed after the mock catechism which ritualizes the dialogue, articulates the dyspepsia which ensues the most gluttonous feast, echoing the ennui in the Duke's opening speech ('Enough, no more! / 'Tis not so sweet now as it was before' (I.1.7–8)). Sir Toby's 'I would we were well rid of this knavery' (IV.2.66–7) expresses both the flatulence of the self-indulgent and his self-interested concern for his own position with Olivia.

The playwright proceeds to the terrific centre-piece by stages: we see Maria costuming Feste in a minister's gown, and Feste getting into the part, urged on by Sir Toby. But the three-cornered exchange between

Feste, Malvolio and Sir Toby's congratulatory expostulations ('Well said, Master Parson', as Sir Topas rebukes Malvolio's sex-mad demon) ceases at line 27, and the core of the scene, with its profound dramatic tension, is a scintillating duologue, in which Malvolio, roused from the folly of his fantasy in Act III, moves from statements of simple outrage to something like an affirmation of who he is and what he believes. This credo can have a stunning effect upon the audience – the comic equivalent of Webster's 'I am Duchess of Malfi still' or Lear's 'Aye, every inch a king'. The scene reaches back into the depths of the play, to the primal antipathy between Malvolio and Feste, propriety and comedy, work and holiday, Saturn and Venus, 'Il Penseroso' and 'L'Allegro', first set forth in Act I, scene 5. It revenges the calculating sneers with which Malvolio set out to deprive the Fool of both credibility and subsistence (70–84): his first words had involved an allusion to the Fool's death. Feste triumphs. Or does he? For nothing that is so, is, in the profundity of the paradox at the centre of *Twelfth Night*. The fantastic laughter the Fool generates reaches fever pitch and goes over the top: in a sense it begets its own opposite. For if Feste revels in his final manic spree of trickery and metamorphosis, he also provides the occasion for Malvolio to consolidate himself, affirming his integrity as, simply and singularly, himself – a believer ('I think nobly of the soul . . .' (54)) and, importantly in a play of such heated social conflict, a gentleman. The scene refers back to the 'cakes and ale' set piece confrontation of Act II, scene 3, and retorts against the memorable justification of festive indulgence made there (110–14) with an equally memorable justification of earnest seriousness. To Sir Toby's insulting 'Art any more than a steward?' (II.3.110–11), Malvolio resplendently answers here, in so many words, that, yes, he is a human soul. Sir Toby's sour abdication therefore marks a dramatically appropriate turning-point. After this, the Clown, in song and in a deranging fluctuation between his own person and his role as Sir Topas, displays his talents with vertiginous zest, fooling Malvolio into unconscious gaffes that acknowledge himself a fool (87–8; 108–9), but the acute nervous tension has subsided. Pen, paper and light are solicited by Malvolio, to make an account of himself to Olivia (106–7; 110–13): the third epistle of the play is about to be discharged into the final Act where its reading precedes his coming, a testament of injury. Shakespeare has throughout the play stressed the destabilizing, protean character of comedy, with its ability to catalyse changes by arousing repressed desires – but in Act IV, Malvolio is not destabilized. Rock-solid, secure in himself, the self is reborn out of its confusion. Malvolio emerges from the ordeal by darkness as the first man in Illyria to be restored from his delirium. As if to mark this dignity, the play promotes him in Act V to the elevation of blank verse where before common prose had been his habitual medium.

Act V

In Act IV, the complications turned on the multiple mistaking of Sebastian for Viola: in Act V, the play's catastrophe, Viola resumes that role, and the whole caboodle of mistakes and their consequences is visited on her head in an escalating sequence of explosions. Act V consists of one single cumulative ensemble-scene, which begins with the Duke's unprecedented outing to visit Olivia in person at the gates of her house – a threshold location which reinforces the liminality of this final phase, with its penultimate spasms of delirium before clarification and dramatic resolution. The scene builds through a gradual feeding-in of characters on a rising note of frenzy, first the Duke and Viola, then Antonio (47), then Olivia (95), the Priest (148), Sir Andrew (170), Sir Toby (189), to a near-complete ensemble-scene whose climax comes at lines 205–6, with the exit of the drunken element and the entrance of the boy-twin. The first part of the scene's action is over and the latter part (Malvolio's climactic anti-climax) not begun. The beautiful recognition-scene (215–55) acts as a miniature play-within-a-play, during which, after a burst of initial exclamation, all but two characters become mute bystanders. Time is stilled as the audience holds its breath to catch every cadence of the emergent sea-music, as *Twelfth Night* makes its final modulation into the lyric voice, a duet of mirroring identities, balancing one another in speeches full of rhythmic and verbal symmetries and repetitions. The missing term in the equation having been supplied, the playwright succinctly reassorts the four young lovers into pairs (256–74), transferring Orsino's affections to Viola in the intervals of the subsequent action. Tempo and mood now change again, with Feste's production of Malvolio's irate letter, which he now proceeds to read aloud in such a berserk voice (the Fool playing the madman) that it has to be handed over to Fabian, the prudent 'straightman' who seeks to mollify the Lady. The letter heralds Malvolio's last magnificent ebullition, exclaiming in a phrase which has become through repetition a choric complaint: 'Madam, you have done me wrong; / Notorious wrong' (326–7). In a masterpiece of construction, the Clown's malign ventriloquism of snatches of the counterfeit letter in Act II, Malvolio's persecution in Act IV and his initial attack on the

Clown in Act I, unbearably acquaint Malvolio with the persons and the means by which he has been 'had'. After his snarling exit, the romantic élite closes ranks and prepares for nuptial celebrations. The Duke has the last, as he had the first, spoken utterance of the play.

The final Act, therefore, flows in a distinct threefold rhythm: the first movement percussively loud, with fast tempo, furious activity and a filling stage; the second quiet and concentrated, with static and spell-bound figures, generating an atmosphere of wonder; the third swirling with renewed activity, further outbursts of rage, and a final exit of all but the Clown, who gives the soliloquistic 'dying fall' to the whole drama. Nervous tension is high throughout, and whipped up by the playwright to a succession of peaks, each of which detonates the next, so that Antonio's ranting wrath with 'That most ingrateful boy' (75) seems to beget a similar rhetoric in the Duke (123 ff.). His extraordinary and apparently out-of-character irruption into a rage which considers murdering first Olivia, then Viola, reads as if it had been pumped up mechanically by Shakespeare for the occasion, but on-stage this is rarely noticeable, for headlong tempo drives the action along from diversion to diversion. Breakneck pace must be remorselessly maintained so that nobody on-stage or in the audience has a chance to pause and think: for instance, after Antonio's accusation of Viola (70–90), the interrogation begun by the Duke ('When came he to this town?' (91)) is aborted by the arrival of Olivia ('But more of that anon' ((98)). Otherwise the cat would be out of the bag, and the dramatist wants to keep it *in* the bag (if detectably mewing) for at least another hundred lines. The dizzy threefold tug of war between Orsino, Viola and Olivia (Orsino trying to drag her off to be made into mincemeat; Viola doing her loving and obedient best to comply; Olivia trying to detain her problematic 'husband') is mediated in a whirling scene of formal couplets reminiscent of the dervish momentum of Act III, scene 1. All three combatants scramble for control of the poetic form, which they break up into halves or thirds:

ORSINO	*Come, away!*
OLIVIA	*Whither, my lord? Cesario, husband, stay!*
ORSINO	*Husband?*
OLIVIA	*Ay, husband. Can he that deny?*
ORSINO	*Her husband, sirrah?*
VIOLA	*No, my lord, not I.*

(V.1.140–43)

Olivia fights for the rhyme that fulfils the couplet *away!/stay!*: to appropriate the couplet form is to acquire 'Cesario' and pair off with him. She builds on her advantage by completing the Duke's floored 'Husband?' in her own triumphant blank verse line. The Duke now turns snarlingly towards 'Cesario', who in turn denies Olivia possession of the couplet by completing it in the negative: *deny?/not I.* With the Priest's arrival, the communal brain-storm slackens, as he delivers himself of a solemn confirmation of the vows attributed to 'Cesario' and Olivia. Sir Andrew's entrance, bawling hysterically and accusing Viola of savage assault, followed by Sir Toby, battered and reeling-drunk, complete the condemnation of Viola by the entire nobility of Illyria, plus Antonio. In lieu of any other channel of relief, Sir Toby whacks Sir Andrew with hateful words of rejection (203–4): silence. This silence is Sir Andrew's final word in the play, and it is eloquent, registering hurt and, perhaps, the aghast recognition that his friend was no friend. The silent knight limps off the stage, perhaps in the opposite direction to Sir Toby – the first of three odd-men-out (Antonio and Malvolio being the others) for whom the Illyrian celebrations have no place. Putting his hand tentatively to the buttery bar, the amiable clodpoll found himself milked dry. The party world is for insiders only, bearing passports of rank, beauty, wit and the talent to play to the gallery and go with the stream. In the delicious conclusion of the play, shadows obscure the interstices between the young people inhabiting the radiant romantic glow.

The arrival of Sebastian (206) radically alters mood and manner. Audience relief is accompanied by the stirring of new suspense, for emphasis moves from *what* will happen now to *how* it will happen. The dramatist feeds joy slowly and lingeringly to his audience and comprehension to the protagonists, together with a sense of blessedness and mystery which looks towards the recognition-scene in *The Winter's Tale*. The scene is an adroit and cunning piece of stagecraft. When Sebastian enters, at first he sees and addresses only his betrothed, Olivia; preoccupied as he is with the thrashing he has just dealt out to his uncle-in-law-to-be, Sir Toby, he remarks that he would have had no alternative 'had it been the brother of my blood' (207), an unsubtle stage-irony that leads in directly to the tableau which begets the Duke's famous exclamation:

> *One face, one voice, one habit, and two persons!*
> *A natural perspective, that is and is not.*
>
> (V.1.213–14)

Perspective glasses (mentioned again at lines 262–3) were a popular newfangled Renaissance toy, distorting or multiplying the object of perception by light-refractions in a manner which (as artists were not slow to grasp) resembled the *trompe-l'oeil* tricks of the trade practised by all the sister-arts, including literature, and especially the drama. The pretence that fraternal twins, let alone two actors, can be identical, is in itself *trompe-l'oeil* illusionism: Jonson asserted that he had avoided the Plautine twin-plot precisely because of the impossibility of finding credible actors. Shakespeare demonstrates the power of the illusion to convince an audience that what self-evidently *is not*, *is* (in the drama) uncontroversially so. The 'natural perspective' so wondered at by the Duke is not, of course, 'natural' at all, but an imitation on an artificial stage: the communal exhalation of wonder by the circle of incredulous witnesses (first the Duke, then Antonio, then Olivia) at once mediates the strangeness and authenticates the dramatic reality of the event. Viola says nothing for twenty-two lines after her brother's entrance: her eloquent silence holds her in reserve for the climax of the scene, until Sebastian's attention has moved from Olivia to Antonio (215–17) who redirects it to his sister (219–21). The core of the scene is in the uninterrupted duologue between brother and sister (223–55), a sequence of eight speeches in which breathless queries and verbal tokens of identity are exchanged in a mutual testament of their joint origins. Sebastian's 'Do I stand there? I never had a brother;' (223) expresses a haunted fear of the *Doppelgänger* or *alter ego*: a climactic expression of the self-mirroring disorientations of the play, staging in its most literal form the shock of being 'beside' or 'beyond oneself', 'out of one's mind'. But the sequence works towards comic *katharsis* of the *Doppelgänger*-complex of the play's many narcissists: however alike we may look, we are different and separate, and in that singleton-state lies the foundation of relationship and bonding. The scene distinguishes self from other, subject from object, illusion from reality. In this dissection, something is lost – the vivid strangeness of the Illyrian life of representation and substitution, with its dream of androgyny and its punning flow of ambivalent language. The twins are delivered from the protean sea to the mainland of norms and conventions.

SEBASTIAN   *Do I stand there? I never had a brother;*
               Nor can there be that deity in my nature
               Of here and everywhere. I had a sister
               Whom the blind waves and surges have devoured.
               Of charity, what kin are you to me?
               What countryman? What name? What parentage?

VIOLA   *Of Messaline. Sebastian was my father.*
            Such a Sebastian was my brother too.
            So went he suited to his watery tomb.
            If spirits can assume both form and suit
            You come to fright us.
SEBASTIAN   *A spirit I am indeed,*
            But am in that dimension grossly clad
            Which from the womb I did participate.
            Were you a woman, as the rest goes even,
            I should my tears let fall upon your cheek,
            And say, 'Thrice welcome, drowned Viola.'
                            (V.1.223–38)

On the face of it, Sebastian's denial of that 'deity in my nature' (of ubiquity) is only a way of affirming the commonplace that human life has to be lived in the singular, but the poetry reverberates beyond the speaker's intention: ironically it is contradicted by the figure of Viola who has 'doubled' for him, living a plural and ambivalent life, here and everywhere in the drama, all things to all people. More elusively, the speech conjures into the recognition-scene the presence, by allusion, of 'deity'. This sense of the holy is increased by the suggestions of death and resurrection implied in the description of a 'sister / Whom the blind waves and surges have devoured', a line so rich in dramatic and poetic suggestions that it seems to reach back into every part of the play: to the dreamlike first speeches of Viola with the Captain (I.2); the strange sea/digestion imagery favoured by Orsino (I.1.9–14; II.4.99–100); the emblematic 'blindness' of Fortune, typically a blindfold figure doling out bounty at random with one hand and blight with the other (Hamlet's 'slings and arrows'), often depicted against a seascape with halcyon weather and fair sailing on her right and shipwreck on her left. In the rich multivalence of Renaissance iconography, however, the 'blind' sea has its own power of transformation: it also represents the medium from which Venus arises, together with her blindfold child Eros, the 'lovely boy' whose role Viola has imitated in the play. Justice herself is blindfold, without respect of persons: in Act V, she appears as poetic justice, rewarding the play's élite with golden gifts.

Just as by excluding 'deity', Sebastian paradoxically invokes it, so the dramatist blurs the distinction between living and dead, ghost and mother's solid child, through a cunning art which has functioned throughout the play to let us have the cake we have already eaten. We know that Sebastian is no 'spirit' returned from the grave, and yet to name such a possibility ('A spirit I am indeed') is in a real sense to entertain it: we are made to sense, through this *trompe-l'oeil*, or rather *trompe-l'oreille*, the numinous proximity of the spirit-world. As brother meets sister, soul meets soul, as if each had passed through the wall of flesh and met at source and destination, where there is no time 'neither male nor female, bond nor free'. In Sebastian's second speech, he gives himself second birth 'from the womb'; recurrently they retrace their steps back to origin and bring themselves home to and in the present moment, where tears are as due as smiles, in token of all that has been lost and found. Many gracious details repeat the motif of re-identification after long loss: 'I should *my* tears let fall upon *your* cheek' ((237), emphases added). We can picture the embrace which makes weeping mutual and signs of sorrow tokens of rapture. The actual embrace is not only dramatically delayed, but remains a prospect to come which is never in fact gratified for the spectators, who thus enjoy the luxury of expectation – the sense of 'something ever more about to be'. The crucial testimony of identity is the fact of the father's death on the sister's thirteenth birthday: some readers link this detail with the symbolic treatment of puberty and adolescence, regarding the whole drama as an initiation-rite, playing out the dizzy disorientations of the quest for identity as the young move from childhood roots over the threshold towards incorporation in the community (symbolized by marriage). The father's loss is at the heart of the scene, strengthening the sense of elegy at the heart of joy (see pp. 53–7 below). Viola's 'Do not embrace me, till ... I am Viola' (248–50) puts off the embrace we have been looking forward to: the taboo echoes the haunted 'out-of-body' suggestions of the whole play. Neither is the return to female clothes, the normative sign of the 'true' identity, completed. Viola retains for Orsino, in suspended transition, and forever, the arrested image of the 'lovely boy' who first beguiled him, 'Boy' and 'Cesario' to the end. The 'initiation-rite' theory takes no account of this licensing of the illicit in the fantasy marriage of man and boy; not only does Jack get his Jill but Jack shall have his 'Jack' and (in the marriage of Olivia with Viola's double) Jill her 'Jill', under cover of social orthodoxy.

The outsiders wander off, however, excluded from the romantic and dynastic bonding that concludes the major action. Malvolio storms out. Antonio is ignored after the recognition-scene: his silence after line 221 can be read as a sign of bitterly painful rejection and estrangement. Like the earlier Antonio of *The Merchant of Venice* he survives in a world where heterosexual bondings are the social norm, and where those who cannot pretend to conform have no place. Finally, the Fool is left to sing alone, a rehash of an old ballad, a snatch of which Shakespeare would later give to Lear's Fool on the Heath. Feste's final statement is the jaded chronicle of an outsider, the entertainer whose presence from birth-day to terminus is an improvised matter of survival in a criminalized riff-raff on the far rim of acceptability. 'But that's all one, our play is done, / And we'll strive to please you every day.'

2. Music and Melancholy

'Bitter-sweet' is a flavour much relished in art, and just as the Chinese have a taste for sweet-and-sour dishes that stir the appetite in ambidextrous appeal to yin and yang, so western tradition has favoured the indulgence of melancholy as a stimulating ingredient of pleasure and beauty. Milton's 'Il Penseroso', written thirty years after *Twelfth Night*, would feed his ear upon the nightingale's tale of mutilation and loss:

> Sweet bird that shunn'st the noise of folly,
> Most musical, most melancholy!
>
> (61–2)

Everyone knew Ovid's legend of Philomela, the raped and muted girl transformed into the bird that fills the night-air with heart-thrilling wordless eloquence. The soul of Renaissance music was this calculated *dolor* on a variety of lachrymose themes – the cruel beloved who rejects the lover; old age bereft of the vigour of youth; separation and mourning – all transformed to meditative beauty, graced with 'dying falls'. Sweet pangs, tormenting joys, lively death and deadly life raised oxymoronic traumas to the power of ecstasy, both in the Petrarchan sonnet and the Italianate madrigal. This same tradition of musical melancholy was passed down to reach the ear of Keats sitting at his window and hearing the nightingale 'pouring forth thy soul abroad / In such an ecstasy!' ('Ode to a Nightingale' (VI.57–8)) and again in his 'Ode on Melancholy', 'aching Pleasure nigh' for whom to 'burst Joy's grape against his palate fine' (III.23; 28) was, by fiendishly difficult tongue-endeavours, to flood the palate with the rich deliquescence of the essence of life fully tasted. Keats was still in touch with the living tradition shared by Shakespeare and Milton, and theorized in Burton's *The Anatomy of Melancholy* to the effect that the melancholic man, saturnine because his nativity is governed by the astrological influence of the planet Saturn, and subject to various constitutional disorders both gastric and mental, is the one best placed for the pursuit of wisdom. Under the old elements and 'humours' system of medicine, the melancholy man suffered from a surplus of black bile which, while it induced various liverish complaints and bilious moods, also rose as spirits to the brain where it brewed deep thought and inward reflection. Dürer's tenebrous woodcut, *Melancholy*, shows her seated in ponderous depressiveness, staring down, while all around her are gathered the tools of her trade, from astrolabes to geometrical instruments: dead to the material world, she is alive to purer knowledge, seeing things in their causes. Above all she is associated with astronomical knowledge, and hence with music – for Dürer's *Melancholy* is pre-Newtonian, in touch with the Pythagorean music of the spheres, the universe being composed upon an octave, inaudible save to the most abstracted minds which may be either the most philosophic, or (in the Platonist tradition) those possessed by the divine *furor* of love.

Shakespearian comedy and tragi-comedy play upon this archaic connection: the harmony they establish is in accord with the sphere-harmony. In *As You Like It*, heaven and earth 'Atone together' (V.4.107), that is, they are at one, in the music of the concluding marriages; in *The Merchant of Venice*, Lorenzo and Jessica sit in the spell of night-music while he teaches her:

> There's not the smallest orb which thou beholdest
> But in his motion like an angel sings,
> Still quiring to the young-eyed cherubins;
> Such harmony is in immortal souls,
> But whilst this muddy vesture of decay
> Doth grossly close it in, we cannot hear it.
>
> (V.1.60–65)

Pericles hears it in Act V of his pilgrimage; and to music Hermione is resurrected (*The Winter's Tale* (V.3.98)). This Pythagorean–Platonist conception of the underlying music of creation brings true married lovers, who make of two bodies one flesh and a mutual mind, to the semblance of a microcosmic harmony, which is the ideal towards which Shakespearian romantic comedy tends. Trapped however in 'this muddy vesture of decay', the lovers of the plays, blinded by Cupid and straying from illusion to illusion, forsaken by the beloved, thrown off by father, cut off from twin brother or otherwise displaced, disowned and all at sea, are far from such perfection. The music of their lyric yearnings resembles a maze or labyrinth of sound, such as Milton described in 'L'Allegro', 'In notes, with many a wandering bout / Of linkèd sweetness long drawn out / . . . The melting voice through mazes running' (139–40; 142). By Milton's time, the madrigal with its complex polyphonic part-singing, was in decline: it had been imported in the 1580s from

Italy, and was at the height of its popularity when Shakespeare wrote that 'maze' of melting voices, *Twelfth Night*. The heroine of the play is named after a musical instrument (and a flower). The viol, either singly or in consort, was used, like the lute, to accompany solo voice or voices, parts being often written so that they could be sung or played interchangeably, each a haunting evocation of the other. Viola's qualification for entry into the Duke's household is her musical accomplishment: 'for I can sing / And speak to him in many sorts of music' (I.2.68–9), that is, she both sings and plays. In point of fact, she never literally does (in our hearing). Or does she? Voice and verse in Renaissance musicology are twin sisters or married partners: the poet as well as the musician is an Orpheus-figure, breathing concordant life into inert and random matter. Manipulating sounds in time, he uses rhythm, pitch, decoration, echo and repeat, dynamics and tempo to attune and temper the ears of the listener. By felicitous phrasing and intonation, expressive utterance and pleasing modulations of rhythm, form and mood, he seeks at once to rouse and calm the mind. 'So as Amphion was said to move stones with his poetry to build Thebes, and Orpheus to be listened to by beasts', so our English poets, said Philip Sidney have civilized England (*An Apology for Poetry*, p. 96). If poet and musician are one – as Viola implies, if 'music' 'speaks' – then language sings, and *Twelfth Night* is all music, not solely its quintessential songs but also the melodious recitative of its language in the higher poetic register, and the festive vernacular of the lower plot, sauced with ballads, catches and rounds. The elaborate interweaving of the plotting through complex knots of complication, as well as the anagrammatic namings (plangently echoic or sharply antiphonal), spin intricate patterns of likeness and unlikeness very close to Renaissance theory and practice of music as *concordia discors* or *discordia concors*.

Illyria is the place not only of *illness, illusion, delirium*, but also of *lyricism*, the *lyre*. Its lyricism is both the expression of malaise and a remedial syrup for it: set your ailments to music (as the Duke proves) and you can enjoy them to the full. *Twelfth Night*'s lyricism orchestrates the communal delirium into a polyphonic form whose unity can only be fully understood after the last note has been played. The elaborate part-song distributed among the voices in the aristocratic plot plays upon a chime of Italianate names – OLIVIA, VIOLA, MALVOLIO – displaying a subtle notation based on anagrammatic and emblematic likeness and deviance, suggesting (as the Clown remarks and nobody takes any notice) *all is one*. OLIVIA is a juggled VIOLA plus the letter 'I': the one signifying the olive of Venus, the other the stringed instrument and the spring flower with its musical-instrument-shaped face and its emblematic association with new life. MALVOLIO contains VIOLA and scrambles OLIVIA. His name may signify 'bad will' and hers be associated with an ultimate peace, but as things turn out they have much embarrassingly in common. They begin as melancholics, fellow-Saturnians – she veiled and mournful, he black-suited, all sombre sobriety. From Saturn they convert to Venus, losing their wits at approximately the same pace, in the havoc of girl-fixation on the one hand and yellow stockings on the other – for yellow is Venus's colour. MALVOLIO scrutinizes in Act II the cryptogram of his name, M.O.A.I: a couple of letters the wrong way round present an identity-puzzle in a code over which he laboriously pores: '"A" should follow, but "O" does . . . And then "I" comes behind' (II.5.127–8; 131). These maladroit deliberations lead to the saturnalian heart of the play's echoing themes – the narcissistic lack of self-knowledge, the communal state of illusion, so that all are mirrors inverting a reflected image – dispossessed selves ('ourselves we do not owe' (I.5.300)) chasing fugitive images projected on to other people by their own wish and desire. If VIOLA is the musical instrument on which a multiple harmony is wrought, MALVOLIO does his name and humour proud by distempered resistance to a place in the communal music. An embodied discord stomps off the stage at the end, implacably and wonderfully himself: 'I'll be revenged on the whole pack on you!' (V.1.375).

'If music be the food of love, play on . . .' If the drama is a linguistic emulation of music, Orsino's direction to the musician is also the playwright's initiating gesture to the play to 'play on', and a direction to the audience as to what to expect. The Duke's mellifluously flowing English with its elegant cadences and balanced phrasings, its modulations between moods and its self-conscious awareness of prosodic shape, pauses and breathings, is therefore the most important index of how the listening ear is to attune itself to the entertainment. Producers who highlight Viola's role by transposing the order of the first and second scenes, substituting Viola's inquiry 'What country, friends, is this?' (I.2.1) for Orsino's opening words about music, forsake this introductory scoring which foregrounds performance-art as a primary subject and not a transparent medium of *Twelfth Night*. The key-subject of the play is not Viola's quest; it is the theme of music – so Shakespeare's original text insists. Orsino's first speech also suggests to the audience's ear the *kind* of musicality to listen for:

> *If music be the food of love, play on,*
> *Give me excess of it, that, surfeiting,*
> *The appetite may sicken, and so die.*
> *That strain again! It had a dying fall.*
> *O, it came o'er my ear like the sweet sound*
> *That breathes upon a bank of violets,*
> *Stealing and giving odour. Enough, no more!*
> *'Tis not so sweet now as it was before.*
> *O spirit of love, how quick and fresh art thou,*
> *That, notwithstanding thy capacity*
> *Receiveth as the sea, nought enters there,*
> *Of what validity and pitch soe'er,*
> *But falls into abatement and low price*
> *Even in a minute. So full of shapes is fancy*
> *That it alone is high fantastical.*

(I.1.1–15)

The speech falls into two distinct passages, the notation for which is written into the form and matter. The couplet at lines 7–8 concludes the equivalent of a sonnet octet, in which the speaking voice negotiates a dialogue with the musician where playing interweaves with language until it is here instructed to break off. So the first half is partially accompanied; the second, which moves into another rhetorical key, is unaccompanied voice. The lyrical octet is a mimetic exercise in which language seeks to vocalize the techniques by which the musician achieves his emotive effects – the susurration of the wind over the violet bank in *sweet sound / breathes / stealing*; the breath-pauses in the phrasings *it#that#surfeiting*; mimesis of the 'dying fall' effect in the end-stopped rhythms of *so die*, and again, *dying fall*. It is not enough to gloss a 'dying fall' as the Arden editor does, as a 'final cadence (with diminuendo?)': this blurred interpretation reminds us of how governed is our musical taste by the intervening four centuries of classical, Romantic and modern musical practice. The 'dying fall' was a quite specific technical device, vital to the ayres, balletts and madrigals of the Elizabethan collections, in which the melodic curve moves characteristically upward to a graceful peak, in order to descend conclusively to the lowest or one of the lowest notes in the range. The languishing rhythm achieved by this device and its repetition may be illustrated in Campion's haunting setting of his own ayre:

Follow your Saint, follow with accents sweet,
Haste you, sad noates, fall at her flying feet.

The sensitive adaptation of prosodic rhythms to musical rhythm is not
only one of the techniques of Elizabethan vocal music; it is also one of
its subjects. Campion's ayre uses the 'dying fall' to express the wistful
love-melancholy of his text; reciprocally, that text contemplates its own
musical form as the subject of the lyric. The *accents sweet* which are
literal echoes of the fugitive Lady's sweetness, are *sad noates* which
(metrically) *fall* at her feet, prostrating themselves at the supine conclusion of every line. Hence the 'dying fall' is both mode and subject of the
poem. Likewise in *Twelfth Night* Orsino's lyricism meditates *itself* and
by extension describes the total melodic arc of the bitter-sweet experience of the play to come: twofold, threefold, fourfold, fivefold love-
languishings as Orsino pines for Olivia, Olivia for Viola, Viola for
Orsino, Malvolio for Olivia, Antonio for Sebastian (even Sir Andrew
for Olivia). Over and over again, variations upon the same key-signature
and musical cadence are repeated, at every pitch from *altus* to bass and
in every mood, from passionate to parodic. In Orsino's 'O it came o'er
my ear like the sweet sound', the 'O' recalls one of the semi-tonal sighs
which helped breathe mood into Italian and then English madrigal
writing; likewise later in Viola's 'Prove true, imagination, O prove true'
(III.4.366). My guess is that Shakespeare intended a wind-instrument
(rather than a lyre, viola or consort) to open the play: this would give
elegant point to the *music / breath / breeze* imagery in which he conceives
the reciprocal relationship between music and ear. Both speaking voice
and musical instrument involve the exhalation of air; sound is taken in
as inspiration (literally, breathing-in) to the creative and transforming
inner world of the 'high fantastical' lover's mind (elaborated in the
second part of Orsino's speech).

   This opening speech should set the tenor of the play as non-realistic.
A musical play will reflect on music, musicians and music-lovers; actors
will impersonate people who reflect upon acting and role-play; intricate
patterns of relationship will address patterns of mimesis. Despite its
vernacular underplot whose colloquial English will persuade us that
we know these speakers or people like them, the total manner of

Shakespeare's Illyria, with its stylized vein of lyricism and its absorption in mimesis, suggests a subtle aestheticism rather than a peep through the window into somebody else's great house. Sir Toby imagines the comic glory of a life lived solely through the medium of dance (I.3.118–26) and all the play's texts and messages are instantly convertible to acting scores, while people are represented as literary texts (I.5.222). In *The Winter's Tale*, Florizel's admiration of all Perdita's graces engenders the desire to turn her whole life into an art-form:

> *When you speak, sweet,*
> *I'd have you do it ever; when you sing,*
> *I'd have you buy and sell so, so give alms,*
> *Pray so, and, for the ord'ring your affairs,*
> *To sing them too; when you do dance, I wish you*
> *A wave o'th'sea, that you might ever do*
> *Nothing but that † move still, still so,*
> *And own no other function.*
>
> (IV.4.136–43)

Still, still so: tranquil eternity in the moving moment of performance is perfectly realized in the balanced musicality which holds the poise and sway of Perdita's being in a heaven of endless repetition, extemporizing the abundance of Florizel's insatiably admiring love, and its tender reverence. Orsino's aestheticism, of course, is nothing like this. Whereas Florizel can never have enough of the real thing, so perfect in its naturalness that it emulates the consummation of art, Orsino's appetite endlessly palls on love-substitutes. But they have in common the matrices of aestheticized worlds – the one of 'golden' pastoral, the other of Petrarchan lyricism, as set to music by the great exponents of madrigal and ayre of the 1590s – Morley, Weelkes, Kirbye, Wilbye, Farmer, Bennet.

However, if *Twelfth Night* is fabricated as a musical play, whose concerns are primarily aesthetic, it is also true that this quality derives from the musicality of social life in the late Elizabethan Great Hall and, indeed, private chambers. Wherever the aristocracy, gathered, and on all royal, civic and dynastic celebrations, there would be music (madrigal, ballett, consort-song, dance-song, ayre, masque-song): the craze for music in the 1590s extended into the social entertainments of not only the rich but also the *arrivistes* and middle classes. *Twelfth Night* was composed on a cresting wave of music-publication: two volumes of John Dowland's *Bookes of Songes or Ayres* (1597 and 1600); Morley's *Madrigalls to Foure Voices* (1594), *The First Book of Ayres* (1600), *The First Booke of Consorte Lessons* (1599) which has an instrumental arrangement of the tune of 'O mistress mine'; Robert Jones's *The First Booke of Songes or Ayres* (1600), Thomas Weelkes' *Madrigals* (1597), and many more. Madrigals proper, and other forms of part-song, were often printed so that the singers could sit round a table to read their parts from the same score at different angles – printed, that is to say, literally at cross-purposes. All the voices have equal importance but each takes a discrepant point of view, making much use of expressive illustrations of the words and of points of free imitation between the voices. This principle of *imitation* in madrigal is of interest because of its highly stylized formalization of exuberant or regretful conflict between the parts: short musical phrases are passed from one voice to another at different melodic levels, frequently with inversion. Einstein wrote of a Willaerts madrigal that 'The singers seem to snatch the single words from one another's mouths.' Whereas Feste's solo songs in *Twelfth Night*, probably sung to lute accompaniment, reflect the plaintive English ayre, these may be regarded as the expressive decorations – melisma – on the polyphonic structure of the play. Indeed, the formal play of voice upon voice in the maelstrom of the final Act shows just this quality of *imitation* in part-song, in which key-words are 'snatched' from mouth to mouth:

OLIVIA	*Ay me, detested! How am I beguiled!*
VIOLA	*Who does beguile you? Who does do you wrong?*
OLIVIA	*Hast thou forgot thyself? Is it so long?*
	Call forth the holy father!
ORSINO	*Come, away!*
OLIVIA	*Whither, my lord? Cesario, husband, stay!*
ORSINO	*Husband?*
OLIVIA	*Ay, husband. Can he that deny?*
ORSINO	*Her husband, sirrah?*
VIOLA	*No, my lord, not I.*

(V.1.137–43)

First Viola heatedly plucks *beguiled* from Olivia's mouth; then *husband* goes the distraught fourfold rounds of three voices, soprano, treble and bass. Frye's remark in *A Natural Perspective* about the closeness of Shakespearian comedy to opera (especially Mozartian opera, *The Marriage of Figaro* and *The Magic Flute*) was not fanciful: the first Italian operas were only a decade away. Thirty-nine years later Milton was to be present at the first *commedia musicale* in Rome, Virgilio Mozzochi's *Che soffre, speri*, with libretto by Rospigliosi. Musical form has entered into the very structure and substance of *Twelfth Night*, from its highest and most refined notes to the *basso profundo* of the world below stairs, where, as soon as conversation gets into its stride, talk is of the arts: 'He plays o'the viol-de-gamboys', remarks Sir Toby of Sir Andrew, a straight lie (I.3.23–4); 'I delight in masques and revels sometimes altogether . . . I can cut a caper' Sir Andrew assures him (107–8; 114). In the drunken scene, Feste's 'O mistress mine' ushers in an action in which the characters converse both by speech and song as the whim takes them, including five popular ballads (II.3.75–8; 83) and a garbled version of 'Farewell, dear heart' from Jones's *First Booke of Songes or Ayres*, sung as a round and designed to mock and needle Malvolio. Later, in the dying moments of the great scene of the persecution of Malvolio, the Clown continues this musical flagellation by singing snatches of Sir Thomas Wyatt's 'Hey Robin, jolly Robin', punctuated by Malvolio's hectic chorus of 'Fool!' which Feste pretends not to hear but which becomes incorporated into the song as a self-rebounding ironic refrain:

> FESTE (*sings*) *Hey Robin, jolly Robin!*
> *Tell me how thy lady does –*
> MALVOLIO *Fool!*
> FESTE (*sings*) *My lady is unkind, perdy.*
> MALVOLIO *Fool!*
> FESTE (*sings*) *Alas, why is she so?*
> MALVOLIO *Fool, I say!*
> FESTE (*sings*) *She loves another – Who calls, ha?*
> (IV.2.71–9)

Malvolio's delusions about his Lady's love are mocked not only by the content of the song but by the ironic commentary on himself provided by his own cry for help, which, in the manner of the ironic refrains patterned into Elizabethan English songs – the dirge-like fa-la's of 'My love she is leaving' (anon.) – mock as fantastic folly all high hopes. To Malvolio, as to Orsino and Sir Andrew, 'My lady is unkind', the one Petrarchan situation (fundamentally an 'art'-situation) dominating the whole play. Both in total structure and in detail, this aestheticism continues, in a system of echoes and antiphonal counter-echoes, to the bitter-sweet end. Thus when Sir Toby comes reeling in for his final drunken expostulations, he badly needs medical attention, which is unavailable, the surgeon being dead drunk like himself: 'Then he's a rogue, and a passy-measures pavin. I hate a drunken rogue' (V.1.197–8) – alluding to the *passemezzo pavana*, a stately dance but performed double-time, as a teetering inebriate might be said to dance through life. Such fancy foot-work is of a piece with the caper-cutting, ballad-singing prose and poetry which are the artful life of the whole play. And *Twelfth Night* dies in music, in the Clown's final ballad, acquiescent in the public's departure from the art-world for the outside world, and in the mortal brevity of the moments of music in 'the wind and the rain' of everyday.

Upon her first entrance in scene 2, Viola inquires of her nautical companions, 'What country, friends, is this?'

> CAPTAIN *This is Illyria, lady.*
> VIOLA *And what should I do in Illyria?*
> *My brother, he is in Elysium.*
> (I.2.2–4)

Viola's question is nearly as poignantly arresting as Orfeo's marvelling exclamations as he enters the Elysian fields searching for his dead wife, in Gluck's opera:

> *O puro ciel! Che chiaro sol!*
> *Che nuova lucè è questa mai!*
> (*Orfeo ed Euridice*, 33)

Viola's arrival also has something of the quality of an afterlife: 'Illyria', as she muses, chimes with 'Elysium'. Shakespeare's setting for *Twelfth Night* is 'Illyria, and another state further along the coast of the Adriatic', but if, having looked it up on a map, you substitute 'This is Eastern Europe, lady', nobody is the wiser. Illyria lies on the wishful borderline between reality and fantasy, speech and music, male and female, loss and comic gratification. It is a foreign country, somewhere 'overseas', where on the face of it they do things differently and see things differently than we do here: in Illyria a girl dressed as a boy can spend three months undetected, though under closest inspection from her male protector and female suitor. In this respect, it is the country of romance convention. Illyrian notables have echoing Italianate names scarcely consonant with Eastern Europe and yet their blood-relatives and acquaintances (Sir Toby Belch, Sir Andrew Aguecheek) enjoy vernacular, allegorical names irreconcilable with those of their supposed kin. Illyria thus incorporates some of the territory of Jonsonian 'humours' comedy. Can Lady Olivia's surname really be imagined as 'Belch', for all her uncle's boasted consanguinity? The synthesis of romantic and 'humours' comedy opens a perspective into a strange foreign land where anything can happen, and simultaneously reintroduces the audience to the home-world of Tudor great houses and estates, a world of domestic interiors with bedrooms, buttery bars, gardens with box-trees and knot-gardens, in a vernacular that was totally familiar, where Englishness (of language, ballad, festive custom, social hierarchy and nuanced class distinctions) is the solid, rooted medium in which the action flourishes. To Viola's dazed question, 'What country, friends, is this?', the Captain might well be giving a coded answer to the effect 'This is England (if you like), lady'. This sense of home-and-garden familiarity links the madrigal-like mazes of cross-purposes and convoluted knots of misidentification not only with musicology (Milton's 'melting voice through *mazes* running' (see p. 35 above)) but also with the Renaissance English love of the labyrinth. Partiality to complicated and intricate patternings in all the arts is evidenced by the Tudor maze as a central feature in gardens – almost a mandala – from the dynastic garden at Nonsuch, with its plethora of knot-gardens and the high-hedged maze of which Anthony Watson said 'you will enter a tortuous path and fall into the hazardous wiles of the labyrinth' (Roy Strong, *The Renaissance Garden in England*, p. 39). In a maze, the wanderer-questor is baffled, disorientated, amused, embarrassed, perhaps a little panicky – in short, amazed. This too is the epitome of the experience of the temporarily deranging, but ultimately delighting, experience of Shakespearian comedy. The Illyria of *Twelfth Night* resembles such a maze, leading to comic *katharsis*, the tension of feeling lost being released as the bemused wanderers suddenly burst into the central heart of the pattern – the great tree at Hampton Court – or else a swelling bank to signify the *mons veneris*. For the maze-quest is also a lovers' journey, the labyrinth of Eros. 'O time, thou must untangle this, not I! / It is too hard a knot for me t'untie' (II.2.40–41), confesses Viola, and plunges back into the embroilment of the conundrum. The 'knot' or maze is, of course, an invention of civilization. The Tudor gardener turned Nature into Art: his virtuoso topiary granted perspectives of conical or animal-shaped trees; his flower-gardens were bright mosaics in which petalled coats of arms or love-devices flourished. It is this art-world of the Renaissance country-house which *Twelfth Night* reflects. Illyria is concerned (unlike the sylvan pastoral of *As You Like It*, the island of *The Tempest*, or the Arcadian Bohemia of *The Winter's Tale*) with culture exclusive of nature – a leisured, tapestried, mirrored world of interiors, contained within panelled rooms behind leaded panes and surrounded by hedged gardens and ancestral walls. The diet is cooked, not raw – cakes and ale, not corn and milk. The air of domesticity which gives the warmth and solidity (the illusion of verisimilitude) to *Twelfth Night* also paradoxically points up the fabricated, aestheticized nature of its experience: both the saturnalian 'downstairs' festivities and the refined 'upstairs' behaviour take place within the context of a civilized world fashioned and decorated to entertain the taste of the dwellers.

Illyria, then, is cultivated ground. The Duke as supreme aesthete of his generation presides at the apex of culture. Renaissance manuals of gentlemanly and lordly behaviour prescribed a musical education as a profoundly desirable acquisition despite the cheap sneers of an old-style élite dedicated to machismo. In Baldassare Castiglione's *The Courtier* (translated by Thomas Hoby in 1561), the Count's praise of music as 'a most acceptable food of the mind' is condemned by Lord Gaspar as a form of effeminacy:

> I believe music . . . together with many other vanities, is meet for women, and peradventure for some also that have the likeness of men, but not for them that be man indeed; who ought not with such delicacies to womanish their minds and bring themselves in that sort to dread death.

The Count retorts with a list of virile pugilists from Alexander the Great to Achilles, whose musical expertise did not dampen their manly thirst for blood. Castiglione makes clear that musical accomplishment, in the form of singing to one's own accompaniment by lute or viola, is not only desirable but necessary to the true courtier, especially in female company. And indeed, the world of Shakespearian comedy, because it is the world of Venus rather than Mars, in which woman 'rules' and man 'serves', tends to be a feminized world, polarizing against the martial Histories. As in Botticelli's *Mars and Venus*, Shakespearian romantic comedy replays the myth of the triumph of Venus over Mars, feminine over masculine, its ethic frankly disgusted with the exploits of the battlefield: 'I pray you, how many hath he killed and eaten in these wars?' inquires Beatrice disdainfully of the boys' games, as the men in *Much Ado* come home from war to a sophisticated world of the emotions they little comprehend and cannot control (I.1.39–40). In *Twelfth Night*, though recall is glancingly made of the sea-battles in which Orsino's nephew lost a leg and Antonio became a buccaneering enemy of the state, this incident subserves the plot, and legs are there chiefly for dancing and for exhibiting in dandified cross-garters. Illyria is not only cultured; it is also feminized. Its ruling classes are represented by a Lady, Olivia; a nobleman Orsino who (to quote Lord Gaspar's sneer) is 'not a man indeed', a girl pretending to be a boy, and two leisured knights who live for indulgence and the bottle. The mover of the underplot is a maliciously witty chambermaid. The 'real men' of *Twelfth Night* are immigrants who cause comic devastation to the music-loving, non-duelling, Illyrians, by bringing in their swords and laying about them.

The cultivated and feminized comic world of *Twelfth Night* assimilates discordancies to its musical harmony. The radiant manner of what is said is often more beautiful and composed than the matter. Comic lyricism fictionalizes pain, cooking it to palatable diet. It brings a sung quality to the most banal or negative of material, from the punning preciosities of the Duke's opening utterances in the 'high fantastical' vein (I.1.15) to the civilized expressions of the Captain to Viola – a sea-captain who has been in receipt of a full humanist education, to judge by his classicizing account of his last glimpse of Viola's brother attaching himself to a mast:

> *Where, like Arion on the dolphin's back,*
> *I saw him hold acquaintance with the waves*
> *So long as I could see.*

> (I.2.15–17)

Tone is craftily light and elegantly nuanced, presenting the classical archetype of the minstrel Arion, master of the lyre, whose salvation from drowning by music-loving dolphins was a prototype of music's power to compose chaos. The analogy is fundamentally relaxing, and 'artificial' in the best sense. On an artful ocean made of graceful word-painting and elegantly buoyant gesture, Viola's brother resembles an emblematic image on a tapestry with a needleworked sea or a framed picture where the swimmer, so urbanely 'holding acquaintance' (rather than grappling with or ploughing through) the element, is unlikely to drown in anything deeper than a layer of paint. The gentleman is on amiable terms with the sea and hardly wet at all; Sebastian is only lost enough to supply a pleasant *frisson* when he turns up. Illyria, and the sea to which it is marginal, is an Orphic world of second chances where bane and privation will (we early begin to trust) ultimately be tuned to heart's ease, as the most plaintive melody finally yields to assent.

Sir Toby (from what we might call the stomach of the play) belches his opinion of the rarefied manners of the melancholics at its heart:

> *What a plague means my niece to take the death of her brother thus?*
> *I am sure care's an enemy to life.*

> (I.3.1–2)

From the third scene, Shakespeare sets up a vigorous contrapuntal bass line, explosively inimical to the tremulous 'dying falls' of tenor, alto and treble. The values affirmed by the 'festive' plot, so ably analysed by Barber in *Shakespeare's Festive Comedy*, is that of Elizabethan holiday and of comedy itself, taking a day off work to eat, drink and be merry, perpetuating the pleasures of the moment until night reels into dawn and not a drop of enjoyment remains to be squeezed out. Sir Toby, sentimentalized by Barber as a Lord of Misrule who is 'gentlemanly liberty incarnate', who 'lives at his ease, enjoying heritage, the something-for-nothing which the play celebrates' (p. 250) is severely dismissed by other critics as a blood-sucking parasite (in Ralph Berry, *Shakespeare's Comedies*, pp. 196–7). Meanly milking Sir Andrew (of lucre, of cheap food for his and our laughter), drinking Olivia's house dry and depriving it of its central pillar, the steward Malvolio, Sir Toby collapses night into day, order into disorder, language into pleasurable anarchy. Most audiences go along with this very readily, up to and a bit beyond the point where enough becomes, unsettlingly, too much. *Twelfth Night* sets up and maintains a constant dialogue and modulation between its lyricism and its uproar – the hungry heart and the insatiable stomach. Sir Toby condemns Olivia's brother-love and the Fool seeks to have her committed for it, within the first Act. The death of brothers is made to seem of small account, dissolved in the sea of alcohol and transformative word-play which can transmute the meaning of any given word into a variant of *what you will*. In the festive lower reaches of Illyria, language has no standardized rigour, but flows like quicksilver along extravagant chains of pun so that undesirables can be wished away in a protean element of wit. 'Care's an enemy to life' is the motto for this pleasure-seeking, pleasure-sharing and pleasure-giving ethos, which is wholeheartedly endorsed by the compulsive belly-laughter in the auditorium.

In Sir Toby's refusal of melancholy lies a dream of freedom:

MARIA   *Ay, but you must confine yourself within the modest limits of order.*

SIR TOBY   *Confine! I'll confine myself no finer than I am. These clothes are good enough to drink in, and so be these boots too; an they be not, let them hang themselves in their own straps.*

(I.3.7–12)

A bill of rights is conferred by the anarchic irregularities potential in language itself: vagrant meanings are substituted for the intended and standardized meaning of any given word: usage licenses behaviour. *Confine* suggests *fine* and *finery*. Sir Toby won't confine himself to sobriety and pretends that a quarrel has been picked with his outfit; then that his outfit has picked a quarrel with himself, thinking itself too fine for his company, whence it comes about that his boots are requested to hang themselves. 'I'll confine myself no finer than I am' expresses Sir Toby's addiction to behaviour and company lower than his rank: his disorderly rascality trades on rank to act the fool at his niece's expense. In developing his puns and *doubles entendres*, Sir Toby reels and veers from the ostensible subject to other subjects suggested by the merest link of sound-similarity. The verbal delight experienced by the audience is produced by the fizzing-up of teeming successions of unrelated images from the initial proposition: we start with the injunction to order and end with suicidal bootstraps. Sir Toby therefore contributes to the 'high fantastical' imaginative field of the play, exposing and exploiting the comic and agreeable disorder within language itself, and doing with it whatever he likes, unrestricted to the tedium of regularized and utilitarian meanings. This is the privilege of the lordly parasite. But the appeal to enjoyment is also an appeal to a certain kind of primary good sense: downright 'cakes and ale' (II.3.112–13), spiced by ginger, as preferable not only to the high horse of office but also to the thin diet of faddy aestheticism. Sir Toby is nearly as hostile to Viola, the Duke's emissary, as to Malvolio (III.1.67 ff.), and takes against the delicate musicality of Sir Andrew's rival's musings, which he apparently overhears:

VIOLA	*Prove true, imagination, O, prove true –*
	That I, dear brother, be now ta'en for you!
SIR TOBY	*Come hither, knight; come hither, Fabian.*
	We'll whisper o'er a couplet or two of most sage saws.
VIOLA	*He named Sebastian. I my brother know*
	Yet living in my glass . . .

(III.4.366–71)

Shakespeare takes care to puncture Viola's exquisite monody with Sir Toby's sneering promise to provide a parody of such arty-farty mood-music. Drawing his companions' attention to the fact that the youth has gone aside and is apparently whispering to himself in rhyming verse, he expresses the pardonable view of the average man *moyen sensuel* upon the high-flown solipsistic flutings that characterize the lifestyles of the Illyrian notability and hangers-on.

An authentic account of *Twelfth Night* must bear witness to the play's laughter, and especially its joyous character, as Hazlitt noted (in Palmer, pp. 29–31): not the blackly indignant, contemptuous mirth of satire which flays its victims as hypocrites and idiots, but rather a cherishing of absurdity which has its effect on the experience of the play at every level. The comic double-act of Sir Toby and Sir Andrew is at the centre of this self-affirming comedy. Sir Toby, the straight-man, nurtures and coddles the fantastic, innocent dim-wittedness of Sir Andrew like a child of his bosom – a child he is always about to expose:

SIR TOBY   Pourquoi, *my dear knight?*
SIR ANDREW *What is* pourquoi? *Do or not do? I would I had bestowed*
                  that time in the tongues that I have in fencing, dancing,
                  and bear-baiting. O, had I but followed the arts!

                                                        (I.3.87–91)

SIR TOBY   *. . . Thy exquisite reason, dear knight?*
SIR ANDREW *I have no exquisite reason, for't, but I have reason good*
                  enough.

                                                        (II.3.136–9)

SIR ANDREW *No, faith, I'll not stay a jot longer.*
SIR TOBY   *Thy reason, dear venom, give thy reason.*

                                                        (III.2.1–2)

Sir Toby feeds Sir Andrew requests for logical explanation as one might feed peanuts to a performing monkey, in the knowledge that his victim has either the most feeble reasons, or none, for his opinions, and the slenderest conceivable grasp of language. His *pourquoi* and his *exquisite* each coerce a laugh from the audience as linguistic eptitude smilingly cozens ineptitude to reveal its empty bag of words. Sir Toby can make Sir Andrew declare himself an ass, speak unconscious bawdry and otherwise give himself away: the laughs are easy because Sir Andrew seldom knows either what he is going to say or the meaning of what he has just said. The constant 'practise' on Sir Andrew is a warm-up for that other puppet, Malvolio. But the effect is not to inspire the audience with disgust at such a dunce: the audience cherishes its victim warmly, and holds out plump cushions to break his recurrent fall into the comic trap. It is Sir Andrew's good fortune to have preserved the innocence of a babe-in-arms as to the vast extent of his own fatuity and openness to insult. Thus, apart from a fog of perplexity which is his native element, and a fierce qualm or two of alarm at having let himself in for a duel with the 'firago', the martial 'Cesario' ('I'll give him my horse . . .' (III.4.279)), Sir Andrew retains until his final whacking by Sebastian and his rejection by Sir Toby, a childlike immunity. It is not so with Malvolio, lacerated to the quick and exposed to public ridicule like a baited bear – and yet the auditorium rings with laughter.

Despite this fizzing brew of laughter, however, it is possible to leave the theatre or close the book with a vague residue of eerie sadness. Or rather, it is less solid than the image of a 'residue' might imply: like the echo of an echo, or the reflection of a reflection, *Twelfth Night* seems to play upon a ghostly key of loss, affliction and deep bewilderment, which sounds through the gentle beauty of romance convention, the modulations between lyric voice and festive humour, as fugitively and elusively as an overheard sigh – or like the respiring of the sea which is heard at intervals on the breath of lyric cadences. From *The Comedy of Errors* to *The Tempest* the sea bereaves and delivers; severs and repairs. Ambivalent symbolic agent of loss and well-nigh miraculous rebirth, its music is the elegy of *mare mater* for the broken trinities or quaternities of blood-kin who, losing one another, lost both self and face:

SEBASTIAN   *I never had a brother . . .*
                  I had a sister,
             Whom the blind waves and surges have devour'd . . .
VIOLA   *Sebastian was my father.*
             Such a Sebastian was my brother too.
             So went he suited to his watery tomb.
                              (V.1.223; 225–6; 229–31)

All drama depends on repetition and echo – of word, act, gesture. The dreamlike reiteration in *Twelfth Night* of the bonded family words – *father*, *brother*, *sister* – each one signifying an absence and loss of security and belonging, and hence of identity itself, achieves a ritual and sacramental quality, at moments a human echo of the Father-Son-Spirit Trinity. The broken triad is rhythmically evoked and invoked at intervals through the play, as part of that pattern of dying falls, its *adagio* music. It is this echo of irreparable loss, and the dream that such loss might after all prove to have been only a dream, which arouses the spellbound sense with which readers or viewers have recorded they left the play, as if they had spent three hours suspended or submerged in reverie: Schubertian *Träumerei* or Fauré's *Après un rêve*.

Through the clear, sleek surface of the lyric mood and the ripplings of the comic manner, an attentive eye can discern that a major theme of *Twelfth Night* is the experience of lack and loss: lack within oneself projected as loss of someone else. There was something, the play intimates, which we once had and without which we are not whole; its people remain, in the absence of this confirmation, haunted, hunting questors, absorbed in the lonely capsule of self but always restlessly on the lookout for the complement that will make them whole. Orsino's languorously insatiable desire for the 'food of love' in the first scene presents a parodic statement of this universal sense of lack in the play, which sets the appetite, eye and ear casting around for gratification it imaginatively constructs and locates. The hunting pun neatly expresses this restless search for wholeness, predicated on the sense of a missing other, which is in turn predicated on an unacknowledged gap where the self should be. Orsino neurotically fails to move out of his room to woo Olivia because there is no self capable of making such a move.

CURIO   *Will you go hunt, my lord?*
ORSINO   *What, Curio?*
CURIO   *The hart.*
ORSINO   *Why, so I do, the noblest that I have.*
         O, when mine eyes did see Olivia first,
         Methought she purged the air of pestilence.
         That instant was I turned into a hart,
         And my desires, like fell and cruel hounds,
         E'er since pursue me.

                                                    (I.1.16–24)

Curio has to repeat his question, for Orsino hears messages from the outside world as more muffled than his own solipsistic broodings. In a play of profound semantic insights, Orsino reveals from the first the privacy of his own linguistic world, whose occult interiority excludes the simple, obvious connections that are real to people who live in the aggregate, consensus reality outside his nervous, super-sensitive and yet arrogant and voluminously wordy mind. To Curio, a representative courtier, a *hart* is a wild creature of the forest to hunt for sport and eat as venison. To Orsino, luxuriously pining for the unavailable satisfactions of a more refined diet, a *hart* (by conventional quibble) is a *heart*, inhabiting inner space. At first we take it that he is hunting Olivia's heart but 'the noblest that I have' is finally identified as his own heart, by assimilation to the myth of the hunter Actaeon, whose unlawful peep at the nude goddess Diana was punished by his transformation into the quarry for his own hunting-dogs to savage and kill; a familiar Elizabethan figure for male carnal salaciousness rebuked by female chastity and one of the commonest emblems to be found on the domestic tapestries and murals of great houses. Renaissance Platonism had allegorized and subtilized the original story of transgression against natural taboo into an intricate fable of man's quest for truth. In Giordano Bruno's fantastical reading of the myth in *De Gli Eroici Furori* published in 1585 and in its English edition dedicated to Sir Philip Sidney, the enthusiast for the divine light is a hunter who is converted into what he hunts: Actaeon and the hounds hunt the mere 'vestiges' of Truth in a world which is only a system of far-fetched 'mirrorings' or 'shadowings' of the Truth. The dogs (allegorized as the 'thoughts' of 'divine things') devour Actaeon who becomes wild like the stag, that is, capable of the mental ecstasy which allows him at last to view the naked Truth. This is fundamentally a Platonist elaboration of Petrarchan conceits such as those which Shakespeare parodies in Orsino.

Twelfth Night elegantly participates not in the philosophical debate but in the analysis of the literary and cultural attitudes which surround it, and the psychology of those attitudes. The study of Orsino is an arresting and not entirely indulgent anatomy of the Platonist and Petrarchan lover, declaring his symptoms with every mouthful of utterance: a man of lovely language, thinking in solitude, and thinking about himself thinking. Cocooned in thought, Orsino is felted with language, for thought nowhere turns to action and therefore devours itself in perpetual and perpetually disappointing suspense. Its idealism is reinforced by its fastidious abstinence from touching the object (Orsino later reveals himself as profoundly misogynistic). Orsino is a neurotically hungry man, who feeds his own famine with airy nothings. He is a lonely man who keeps himself company (until he meets a gentle and ambivalent shadow of himself in 'Cesario') and is not seen to go out until the final Act. He is an unhealthy man in need of healing ('Methought she purged the air of pestilence'), fastidiously aware of bad odours and the need for sweet scents (I.1.5–7). As a person in eternal retreat from himself ('my desires ... / pursue me'), he seeks refuge in the imaginative rather than the active tasting of experience. Such complex neediness is presented through the smooth and harmonized verse that almost cancels what it articulates: this play above all others manifests the Keatsian recipe for poetry as Truth in solution with Beauty, disagreeables made not only tolerable but delightful by loveliness of expression – as well as by the delicate implicit ironies by which they are angled and qualified for the hearer or reader. Contemporaries recognized the lush beauty of the Shakespearian style:

the sweet wittie soule of *Ovid* lives in mellifluous & hony-tongued *Shakespeare*, witness his *Venus* and *Adonis*, his *Lucrece*, his sugred Sonnets among his private friends &c.

Francis Meres, writing in 1598, overdoes the honey and sugar but his link between Ovid and Shakespeare aptly associates transformative style and legends of metamorphosis. Transferred to dramatic character, that honey-tongue which sweetens all it says is made partly to disclose, partly to conceal, the uncertainty and lack at the root not only of Orsino's character but of most of the play's major persons. This is, of course, a lack proper to the Platonist and Petrarchan lover and to the musical tradition whose expressiveness was built on it. Plato's *Symposium*, the dialogue on love which served as a handbook to the Renaissance philosophy of love, identified love as lack: 'it is because he lacks what is good and beautiful that Love desires these very things' (202). Love is a hole, an emptiness, an absence longing to be filled. So *Twelfth Night* is a play of pining: Orsino for Olivia; Olivia for Viola; Viola for Orsino; and, comically, Sir Andrew for Olivia. The comedy is drawn from the symmetrical pinings, the sadness from the sense of lack all the way round the circle, solved only by the rectifying intervention of Viola's male double, a second self that fills the void of identity and remedies the 'lack of what is good and beautiful' in the others. This emphasis on pining invokes the classical myth of Narcissus and Echo (see p. 59 below), and makes up a narcissistic triad of self-enclosed lonelinesses, simultaneously dwelling upon their own reflections in the mirror of others' faces and hearing their own voices echoed where no true compatibility exists. Each reciprocally plays Narcissus and Echo. Orsino loves the image of himself as the lover of Olivia; Olivia loves her own gender in the Viola she cannot perceive in 'Cesario'; 'Cesario' loves 'his' own image in Orsino. Additionally, Antonio pines for his likeness in Sebastian. Each is rejected by the beloved.

More touching than the love-sorrows, perhaps, and yet germane to them, is the theme of the separation of closely bonded blood-kin, by real or apparent death. Here the fine-tuning of the sense of loss recorded by the play refines its subject-matter to the condition of pure beauty, like the plucked, quivering string of a musical instrument, wrought to an acute pitch of perfection. If we stand back to meditate the play as an entire psychological statement by a single mind, the drama may be viewed as aligning that state of primary loss with the sense of romantic lack I have described, as source and issue. Nearly all the characters bear traces of a sense of primary loss, from the doubling of the motif of the loss of father-and-brother in the nearly parallel traumas of Olivia and Viola, right down the scale of romantic and farcical comedy to Sir Andrew's wistfully nostalgic echo of the key-signature in the immortal 'I was adored once, too' (II.3.174), a line which, delivered with due effeteness and determination not to be left out, invariably brings the house down. Yet that echo is finely in tune with the nostalgic experience of loss which opens the play and is maintained throughout (doubled in the cleavage between Antonio and Sebastian) until in Act V the restored twins bring themselves home to one another and repair the gaps and fissures caused by the crises of identity which their separation initiated. The play frequently points backwards to that 'once' when Sir Andrew alleges he was 'adored'. We all were, once. *Twelfth Night*'s music, as Orsino wishes to believe, leads there, to some lost golden time only to be found in compensatory echoes such as Feste's music. Music itself comes to seem a covering for loss. Orsino omnivorously calls for it because it gilds sadness and aestheticizes pain at the same time as it acknowledges their reality. As the 'food of love', it offers a kind of sustenance, answering to the never satisfied need of nurture, a bottom-less pit of need like a child's dependent hunger:

> *Give me some music! Now, good morrow, friends!*
> *Now, good Cesario, but that piece of song,*
> *That old and antique song we heard last night.*
> *Methought it did relieve my passion much,*
> *More than light airs and recollected terms*
> *Of these most brisk and giddy-pàced times.*

(II.4.1–6)

Orsino's song must be *old and antique*, a trace or vestige of some unspecified bygone period which is conceived as an epoch of stability and consistency – in direct contrast to fickle modernity and to his own volatile nature which skims insecurely between one temporary whim and the next. When Feste is located and the song about to be served up, Orsino interpolates a preface (which Viola can scarcely be said to require, as she must have heard the song with him the previous night):

> *Mark it, Cesario; it is old and plain.*
> *The spinsters, and the knitters in the sun,*
> *And the free maids that weave their thread with bones,*
> *Do use to chant it. It is silly sooth,*
> *And dallies with the innocence of love*
> *Like the old age.*

(II.4.42–8)

Old and plain: Orsino credits the song with a nostalgic and folk-ballad Englishness (puzzling in the light of its highly formal lachrymosity) and pointedly ascribes it to the pastoral simplicity of working women's oral music. He goes out of his way to describe the women's trade – weavers and spinners – with their tools and an impression of a summery outdoor location, and he imagines these women singing together in a group as inhabiting a golden age ('the old age'). Things were better once, homelier and more simple. Orsino's yearning conjures up a maternal world of group bondings now forever unavailable – the 'art-world' of pastoral 'nature'. The song that follows, 'Come away, come away, death' with its white shroud and black coffin, echoes the mood of dolorous self-gratification: *lachrymae rerum* drunk as a beverage.

If Orsino, obliquely and subliminally, wants his mother, Olivia and Viola both want a brother and a father. These near-anagrammatical characters reflect one another's life-situations with uncanny exactitude, like a mirror-reversal. They are opposites in the same kind. This opposition is a comic realization of a forsaken condition, for both are recently bereaved, orphaned and brotherless – young women fending for themselves in a male world over which they have tenuous control. Shakespeare's treatment of this intrinsically tragic theme of bereavement has a subtly nuanced lightness, appropriate to the romance genre, which distances the emotion of grief so that we see its vestigial shape without feeling its immediate power to wound: a framed reflection in a pane rather than a shared trauma. Olivia neither mentions her brother nor shows evidence of grief for his loss after the scene in which the Fool proves her a fool for excessively mourning him (I.5.52–67). And the introduction to her brother-loss which establishes an audience-response is at two equivocal removes, in reported speech transmitted by Valentine via 'her handmaid' (presumably Maria), and possibly representing a device for keeping the unwanted attentions of Orsino at a distance:

> *So please my lord, I might not be admitted,*
> *But from her handmaid do return this answer:*
> *The element itself, till seven years' heat,*
> *Shall not behold her face at ample view,*
> *But like a cloistress she will veilèd walk,*
> *And water once a day her chamber round*
> *With eye-offending brine; all this to season*
> *A brother's dead love, which she would keep fresh*
> *And lasting, in her sad remembrance.*
> (I.1.25–33)

Olivia's taking of the veil; her anchoritic self-sequestration and her ceremonial timing of tears, all proclaim a conduct comically in excess of the occasion. Seven years fanatically violates Elizabethan mourning-etiquette, which prescribes a period of one year for a brother. Olivia closely parallels Orsino both in her reclusiveness (though this is rather alleged than borne out) and as a willing victim of introspective melancholia who is backward-looking to the security of the past – Orsino's 'the old age', Sir Andrew's 'once'.

Olivia's unnamed brother (a deep part of her original life and psychology) fades from the surface of the play; but his ghost continues to haunt it, for no sooner has the theme of brother-loss been sounded in the minor key than it recurs in the major. The 'eye-offending brine' of tears gives way to that of the sea. Olivia's brother fades into Viola's, as Viola appears on the stage as the surviving remnant of a boy-girl pairing. These mirroring situations carry a double intimation of primary loss into the play, from its outset. In a drama greatly concerned with wholeness of identity, the twinned heroines are each presented as halves of a pairing, cloven away from the male counterpart with whom she started life. When Viola assumes her male disguise, it is as if she recapitulates in her own person this lost other, and as if Olivia also locates her own in her. The play's sexual ambivalence, with Viola its androgynous centre, presents a rich complex of dramatic and poetic suggestions (see Ch. 6 below). In Jungian terms, it fuses both gender-polarities, animus and anima, in a transgressive wholeness which, by trespassing over the borders of what society constructs as 'male' and 'female' behaviour, seems to recapitulate the lost integration of pre-pubertal life, with its fugitive freedom from the yoke of sex, gender-roles and biological imperatives. That is why Viola is always 'boy', 'youth', carrying to the malingering protagonists the freshness of youth. But it is as an incarnation of her own twin brother that Viola/'Cesario' is most spellbinding. On the stage, the cross-dressing sister impersonates her missing brother, haunting the play during his long absences from view with his immanence. The male costume, role and behaviour feigned by Viola therefore function as a visible sign of loss and compensation for loss. She herself reflects on her time-biding, suspenseful incorporation of her fraternal twin: 'I my brother know / Yet living in my glass' (III.4.371–2). 'Do I stand there?' wonders Sebastian, staring at his mirror-image in the other 'boy' (V.1.223). Uncannily, it is as if the persistence of the illusory Sebastian (Viola) has called the reality by magnetic magic, and under the aegis of the play's artistic Providence, from Elysium to Illyria.

I cannot persuade myself to omit from this account of *Twelfth Night* one pregnant fact of Shakespeare's biography: he was the father of boy-and-girl twins, of whom the boy-twin died before the composition of the drama. The children, Hamnet and Judith, were born in 1585; Hamnet was eleven and a half years old when he was buried at Stratford in the August of 1596. So the theme of *Twelfth Night* was one which

Shakespeare *must* have had very much at heart. I can never read the play without feeling that the Shakespearian music here records in bearable and healing form the unbearable severing of that pair. The wistful, musical sadness of Viola is the face of loss superimposed upon the terrible facelessness of Death: looking into the eyes of Judith, Shakespeare must have seen Hamnet. The surviving girl-twin, about Viola's age when *Twelfth Night* was written, was a mnemonic of the lost features, at once sharply painful in insisting that what she impersonated was lost forever, and remedial in guaranteeing that the imprint and trace of the lost boy would survive as long as she lived. For this reader, *Twelfth Night* contains a calm, loving elegy, and a myth of rebirth. It feigns that the boy-twin is not dead; he lingers in the unknown, washed up on some other shore, in the care of some other's unknown hand. 'Prove true, imagination, O prove true' – the imagination's restorative power holds sway only in Illyria, or Arden, or on Prospero's island, or upon the saturnalian stage itself, where all that *is not*, outside on the globe, *is* incontestably in the here-and-now of the Globe.

Other, later texts which feature a comparable sense of yearning incompleteness in the context of brother-sister love are Romantic versions of the *alter ego* or *Doppelgänger* theme: Byron's twins in *Cain* or the siblings in the 'Epistle to Augusta' ('From life's commencement to its slow decline / we are entwined' (XVI)); Shelley's narcissistic 'Epipsychidion' where the soul-sister is metaphorical kin; Emily Brontë's *Wuthering Heights* ('surely you . . . have a notion that there is, or should be, an existence of yours beyond you . . . I *am* Heathcliff' (Ch. IX)). But the motif has its roots in ancient philosophy and myth, the most appropriate to a reading of *Twelfth Night* being Plato's legend of the original spherical people cloven in half by Zeus for their rebellion and destined forever to run in frantic pursuit of the lost half of the self. This story, told with pleasant levity by Aristophanes in *The Symposium*, was earnestly glossed and interpreted in the Renaissance, most notably by Ficino in his well-known *Commentary on Plato's 'Symposium'* of 1484, which had an incalculably diffusive effect on Renaissance love-literature.

In the first place there were three sexes, not, as with us, two, male and female; the third partook of the nature of both the others and has vanished, though its name survives [hermaphrodite] . . . It is from this distant epoch, then, that we may date the innate love which human beings feel for one other, the love which restores us to our ancient state by attempting to weld two beings into one and to heal the wounds which humanity suffered.

Each of us then is the mere broken tally of a man, the result of a bisection which has reduced us to a condition like that of flat fish, and each of us is perpetually in search of his corresponding tally. Those men who are halves of a being of the common sex ... are lovers of women ... Women who are halves of a female whole direct their affections towards women ... But those who are halves of a male whole pursue males ... Such boys and lads are the best of their generation, because they are the most manly.

(The Symposium, 189e–192)

Plato formulates man's major urge as the longing to 'melt into his beloved', to become 'one being instead of two'. The reason is that this was 'our primitive condition when we were wholes, and love is simply the name for the pursuit and desire of the whole' (192–3). The homoerotic bias reflects the conventions of Plato's world, where the cultural élite of Athens practised a cult of homosexuality, but it has a resonance too for the author of the Sonnets saluting the 'master-mistress of my passion' (20) who stands as 'all the better part of me' (39), and of *Twelfth Night* where the shadowy innuendoes of Lesbian pairing (Olivia and Viola) and pederastic pairing (Orsino and 'Cesario') are stated not only against a key-theme of cloven twins (Sebastian and Viola) but also against a bass chord of alarming intensity in the raw attachment of Antonio to Sebastian:

> *This youth that you see here*
> *I snatched one half out of the jaws of death;*
> *Relieved him with such sanctity of love;*
> *And to his image, which methought did promise*
> *Most venerable worth, did I devotion.*

(III.4.350–54)

This is the most vehement anguish of love postulated in the whole comedy: a passion so aggressively devoted that it assumes a sacrilegious form, investing itself with 'sanctity' and worshipping the graven image of another man's face. In this drama of deceptive shadows and reflections, the word *image* carries a special irony, since Sebastian is only the image of Viola, and vice versa. Antonio corresponds more closely than any other character to the Platonist image of the lover as questor, the stranded half-man obsessively chasing the fugitive likeness of his lost same-sex counter-part, in whom, as Plato says, love inspires 'an emotion which is quite overwhelming, and such a pair practically refuse ever to be separated even for a moment' (192d). It is Antonio's asymmetrical tragedy that his love is destined, in this play of symmetrical heterosexual matings, never to find completion: odd-man-out, he is left to himself as the twins and mates unite, in stunning and equivocal silence (see p. 132 below).

Love in *Twelfth Night* defines itself as a higher narcissism, self seeking to be mirrored in a matching counterpart. The legend of Narcissus and Echo had a more serious and meaningful interpretation in the Renaissance than the degenerate version inherited by later generations, being read as an allegory of the difficulty and partiality of perception of truth in the world of sense-impressions:

The young Narcissus, that is, the soul of rash and inexperienced man, does not notice his own proper substance and qualities, but pursues his shadow in water and tries to embrace it, that is, he admires beauty in a fragile body and in running water, which is a shadow of the mind itself, and turns his back on his own beauty.

(Davies, S. (ed.), *Renaissance Views of Man*, p. 50)

This passage from Ficino's *Commentary on Plato's 'Symposium'* starts from the premise that the world of sense-impressions is a system of shadows and reflections, at one remove from the reality of the Ideas, in which man (a composite of senses and soul) is set the riddle of finding the truth. Ficino does not rebuke Narcissus for being self-obsessed; self-obsession is the *duty* of man. He only regrets that Narcissus seeks himself in shallow and distorting appearances rather than using this partial beauty as a means of finding the fuller mental beauty that leads to fulfilment. The dilemma of the characters of *Twelfth Night* who are hunting themselves is analogous to the dilemma of Narcissus (Narcissus, like Hyacinthus, being commonly read as a homosexual figure). Viola's cross-dressing tells to both Olivia and Orsino a veiled truth; in Act V, Sebastian's emergence draws the veil aside. As her twinned 'other self', he now becomes Olivia's true counterpart, 'flesh of her flesh' in the marriage service; at the same time, he releases Viola to become the 'other self' of Orsino. Homoerotic shades into heterosexual, but the borders are blurred to the very end.

French Renaissance lyricists spoke of love as the search *'de recouvrer sa part et sa moitié'*. In the double marriages which consummate *Twelfth Night*, each containing an identical twin, Shakespeare presents a fourfold consolidation of such recovery: Orsino is linked to Olivia (his initial heart's desire), Olivia to Viola, Viola to Sebastian, Sebastian to Olivia, Orsino to Viola, through this fourfold union of the two couples. Shakespeare doubles the consanguineous doubles in a grouping which forms a *quaternio*, the Renaissance ideal model of wholeness and perfection. In an age fond of playing with numerological symbolism, four was pre-eminently the number of amity and friendship, the two central digits providing the linking terms for the outer:

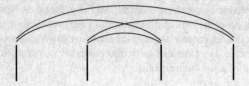

Thus the problems of ambisexuality in the play, as in other romances, are comically resolved in the two marriages, which bond all the lovers into one family, with no individual excluded. Olivia emphasizes to Orsino the new kinship which is also a dynastic alliance:

> *My lord, so please you, these things further thought on,*
> *To think me as well a sister as a wife,*
> *One day shall crown th'alliance on't, so please you,*
> *Here at my house, and at my proper cost.*
>
> (V.1.313–16)

Orsino echoes this in the play's closing moments by addressing Olivia as 'sweet sister' (V.1.381) and seems to embrace all four participants in the final ceremony, for when

> *golden time convents,*
> *A solemn combination shall be made*
> *Of our dear souls.*
>
> (V.1.379–81)

The double marriage is a quadruple pledging of kinship, an interweaving of the four musical parts into one whole. *Convents* means 'come together'; *golden time* implies a restitution of the golden age Orsino spent the play lamenting, whose loss he compensated in the pleasing syrup of melancholy music, and also the *time* that music itself keeps ('We did keep time, sir, in our catches' (II.3.92)). The double marriage that resolves the romantic plot is therefore scored as a harmonious resolution of the cunningly vagrant patterns of a part-song as it yields to long-delayed assent. But the goldenness of this concordancy stands in tension with those embarrassing elements of the play which refuse final synthesis: the continuing maelstrom of Malvolio's bitter and justified indignation vents a final seismic outburst between these speeches and is never resolved; the odd-men-out (Antonio, Sir Andrew, Feste) either wander out or linger in non-duetting jadedness on the margins of the circle of the great ones' happiness, bathed in a little condescending warmth and light. The Clown concludes, inhabiting an eternal and monotonously drenching here-and-now, at the limits of the illusion, reminding the audience that all endings (even, or especially, happy endings, with their inevitable anti-climax) are sad endings, disappointments, alleviated only by the possibility of coming in from the cold for new illusions tomorrow:

> *A great while ago the world began,*
> *With hey-ho, the wind and the rain;*
> *But that's all one, our play is done,*
> *And we'll strive to please you every day.*
>   (V.1.402–5)

3. A Note on Fools

We, who hate to be made fools of, flock to *Twelfth Night* to get the pleasure of seeing imaginary people making fools of one another. Anonymously immune in the audience, we are licensed to kid ourselves that we are not viewing ourselves in a mirror but peeping in through the window at the spotlit, beetroot faces on the stage. The play is as good as its fooling, and the democratizing beam of scorching light cast by the foolers on the fools collapses all their features, together with distinction of class, into one face – that of an ass – and their dialects into a common braying. The foolers one-up on the fools; they extrapolate themselves from the asinine crowd and, calling the tune, display themselves for our admiration as their superiors. We have *carte blanche* to gloat and grin with them, for they are an extension of us and we of them, outsiders in the know, looking on and not taken in. 'Satire', as Swift said, 'is a sort of glass, wherein beholders do generally discover everybody's face but their own.' *Twelfth Night*, of course, is not satire except in the most delicately veiled way (see pp. 89 ff. below) but it does hold up a mirror in which, however, we are not expected or required to recognize our specific selves. The Fool, so central to the play's art, conventionally carried an unflattering glass, which he would whip out and stick in front of people's faces when they were least expecting it, in the wholesome cause of conferring self-knowledge on the victim. Feste's witticisms function in this way, but the play's narcissists, dreamily intent upon viewing their own reflections in mirrors of their own devising, are not impressed. Perhaps, indeed, *Twelfth Night* implies, it is not possible for human nature to profit from its feast of comic advice, however wit-salted and palatable. The possibilities of being bamboozled and hoodwinked seem limitless; every character (with the exception of Maria and Feste) is shown as credulously led by the nose by the play of optical illusions and verbal sleights which are all the comedy knows of reality.

In this drama of many mutual reflections, the fooling of Malvolio acts as a paradigm of the posturing folly that lurks in the depths or shallows of every human animal, at the heart of his aspirations, fantasy-life and notions of his own worth and others' lack of it. The laughter he lacks is at the basis of what *Twelfth Night* coerces or tickles from us, the audience, and asserts as essential to right reason and self-knowledge. The supercilious quarrel he picks with Feste on his first appearance is therefore a quarrel with comedy itself. After his sour reproof of the Fool ('I marvel your ladyship takes delight in such a barren rascal' (I.5.78–9)), which is also a rudely injudicious hit at his employer herself, Olivia delivers her famous diagnosis: 'O, you are sick of self-love, Malvolio, and taste with a distempered appetite' (85–6). His palate for life being tainted by a bilious stomach, the four 'humours' of his body are out of balance (*distempered*), and he lacks proportion. Olivia knows exactly what is wrong with Malvolio and what would prove curative (a dose of Feste). Olivia, however, who can divine and gently rebuke the kind of folly whose symptomatology Malvolio manifests, cannot apply the same forensic eye to her own malaise, which is another strain of the same bug: 'I am as mad as he / If sad and merry madness equal be' (III.4.14–15). She too is severely embarrassed, squirming worse than Malvolio as she besieges the cool boy with her impassioned attentions. The theme of 'distemper' runs all the way up and down the comic chain. All fools together, they swagger, simper, bleat, pull faces, make speeches and inflate until they pop, in the same comic mirror. *Twelfth Night* makes fools of the wisest of its characters and proves its wisest character to be the Fool. It invests for some of the time almost the whole company of actors and by implication the audience (which, however, foolishly disdains to make the connection) with cap and bells, motley and bauble, ass's ears and fatuous physiognomy. Wandering around in a state of deep illusion, Malvolio could be any or all of us at least one day in the year, when we all go about yellow-stockinged, cross-gartered and preposterously smiling, and catch perhaps an agonizing glimpse of ourselves in an accidental shop-window or car mirror. Acute embarrassment is a principal theme of the play; the laying bare of those huge cringing gaffes that are never lived down. Kinder to some (generally speaking, the young, patrician or witty) than to others (puritans and loobies), the play insists on its universal common denominator, *fool*, from Sir Andrew's 'I knew 'twas I, for many do call me fool' (II.5.80) to Feste's catechism of Olivia, 'Take away the fool, gentlemen' (I.5.66–7).

This tradition of 'Folly' parallels the ancient 'Vanity' tradition with its roots in the Book of Ecclesiastes, and the 'Mortality' tradition (symbolized by the *memento mori* such as the skull in *Hamlet* and *The Revenger's Tragedy* which acts as a grotesque warning mirror to what lies beneath the cosmetic mask of pretence and pretension). The Fool as *memento moriae* (reminder of folly) is really a comic version of the *memento mori*: a levelling device which reduces the social hierarchy to a common, dumbfounding equality – common as muck – for the Fool's role is to prove, by a consistent destabilizing policy of linguistic reversal and inversion of norms, that there is nothing to choose between the Lady Olivia and a fool; just as the skull of Yorick demonstrates that there are no odds between Caesar and a bung-hole (*Hamlet*, (V.1.209–10)). In the land of Folly, only the Fool is exempt from the global state of illusion. For his knowledge is that Socratic wisdom inscribed over the shrine of the Delphic Oracle in Ancient Greece: 'Know yourself. Know that you know nothing.' Hence the ancient connection between folly and defective self-knowledge. In *Twelfth Night* the coldly piercing light of the Fool's insight sees straight through the façades of his fellow characters to their hidden calculations (hidden perhaps even from themselves) and to their delusions and irrational sources of behaviour. 'Well, go thy way,' he says to Maria, 'if Sir Toby would leave drinking, thou wert as witty a piece of Eve's flesh as any in Illyria.' 'Peace, you rogue, no more o' that' she quickly chides him (I.5.24–7), hiding her adventurism up her skirts again, where it remains until we learn of her translation into 'Lady Belch' in the last Act (V.1.362). All those who come within the Fool's orbit feel the bale of his anatomizing eye:

ORSINO   *Give me now leave, to leave thee.*
FESTE   *Now the melancholy god protect thee, and the tailor make thy doublet of changeable taffeta, for thy mind is a very opal. I would have men of such constancy put to sea, that their business might be everything, and their intent everywhere; for that's it that always makes a good voyage of nothing. Farewell.*

(II.4.71–7)

Feste calls Orsino *thou* rather than *you*, implying equality and familiarity, and gets away with it in part because his riddles are seldom perfectly understood. They are arrows which whiz at high velocity just past the victim's ear. The Fool exits and the Duke ignores his speech, presumably unaware that he has just been expertly diagnosed. Shot-silk, flowing between variable colours at the whim of the light, would be apt apparel (indeed, a sort of parti-coloured motley) for his volatility. None the wiser, the Duke continues to veer and tack across the trackless seas of his mind.

The humanist revival had made a special place for the 'Folly' tradition, from Petrarch's *On His Own Ignorance and that of Many Other People* (1368), where the Socratic mingles with Gospel admonitions of the mighty and the mightily learned, to Erasmus's *Praise of Folly*

(*Encomium Moriae*) (1511), which passed the 'Folly' tradition to Shakespeare's generation. As a satire on the affectations of theologians, philosophers, princes and pontiffs, it looked down on the antics of the human race from a great height, for from the moon 'you'd think you saw a swarm of flies or gnats quarrelling amongst themselves' (p. 143). In Erasmus's as in Shakespeare's time, licensed fools were kept in great households, a custom that did not die out until 1700. Erasmus points out that fools do more than divert their masters: 'They're the only ones who speak frankly and tell the truth' (p. 118). He comments on their linguistic resources, freeing them from the courtier's ingratiating double-talk: 'a habit of changing black into white and blowing hot and cold in the same breath, and there's all the difference between the thoughts he keeps to himself and what he puts into words' (p. 118). When Olivia rebukes Malvolio by pointing out that 'there is no slander in an allowed fool, though he do nothing but rail' (I.5.98–9), she is echoing Erasmus's reflection that:

[Fools] can speak truth and even open insults and be heard with positive pleasure; indeed, the words which would cost a wise man his life are surprisingly enjoyable when uttered by a clown. For truth has a genuine power to please if it manages not to give offence, but this is something the gods have granted only to fools.

(Erasmus, *Praise of Folly*, p. 119)

One of Holbein's illustrations to Erasmus's book showed the picture of an ordinary-seeming man's head viewed from the back (a common reader, perhaps, one of us), looking into a mirror. From the mirror gawps a fool's face wearing cap and bells, looking back not only at the startled viewer in the picture but also into the mirrored face of the complacent voyeur, over his shoulder. The book is the mirror; the reader the fool. It takes one to see one. So, also, Shakespeare's play, which draws on the Erasmian tradition as well as the stage convention (his company, the Lord Chamberlain's Men, including a professional 'clown' actor, Robert Armin, for whom Feste's part would be directly designed), may be played or read as presenting a composite mirror for both characters and audience. This enlarged frame of reference on the 'all fools together' theme is alluded to by Feste in Act II:

SIR ANDREW	*Here comes the fool, i'faith.*
FESTE	*How now, my hearts! Did you never see the picture of We Three?*
SIR TOBY	*Welcome, ass!*

(II.3.14–17)

This plays on the familiar inn-sign featuring two fools or asses, entitled 'We Three', hence extending a welcome to that other ass, the spectator, just as the play of *Twelfth Night* extends a friendly welcome to its mirrored audience.

The geniality of the jest is close to the spirit of most of *Twelfth Night*, in contradistinction to the more sinister and threatening absurdism of *A Midsummer Night's Dream* which plunges its audience into a communal and hypnotically deep dream – dream-within-dream, the area of the uncanny, where the highest of the high (Titania) becomes besotted with the lowest of the low (Bottom, the weaver, with the head of an ass) and love madly changes partners in frenetic metamorphosis. Folly and madness in *Twelfth Night* are domesticated and aestheticized by comparison: unreasoning fooleries rather than full-blown irrationality. Eros, the blinding, illusion-producing, aggressive god of Love, dominates the action of both plays, producing that state of erotic mania or *furor* which Plato depicted as a state of possession or seizure proper to the state of love, and linking it ambivalently to animal appetite on the one hand and divine insight on the other (*Phaedrus*, 244). By comparison with the scalding lunar frenzies of the lovers in *A Midsummer Night's Dream*, Orsino's imaginative realm of Eros which sets the scene for the later play is a form of cerebration, suspended in the art-world rather than running amok in the night-world of an enchanted forest 'outside Athens':

> *Away before me to sweet beds of flowers!*
> *Love thoughts lie rich when canopied with bowers.*
>
> (I.1.41–2)

Nature's furniture (*beds* and *canopies*) has been sumptuously crafted, with no expense spared (*rich*) into a pictorial artifice, so that stylized flower-beds can elegantly rhyme with over-arching trees (*flowers/bowers*) with artificial preciosity, like a scene in a tapestry, completed by the central emblem of the picturesquely recumbent lover. *Twelfth Night*, unlike *A Midsummer Night's Dream*, views Eros not at its subconscious roots but as it is reflected in fashionable literature and culture. The Erasmian notion of genital folly as the foundation of human madness is not as germane to *Twelfth Night* as is its satire on pretension:

The propagator of the human race is that part which is so foolish and absurd that it can't be named without raising a laugh. There is the true sacred fount from which everything draws its being, not the quaternion of Pythagoras.

(*Praise of Folly*, p. 76)

The nearest the play gets to this perception is the Fool's assimilation of 'a foolish thing' (his phallus) to a 'toy', or fool's bauble, in his final song (V.1.388). The target of *Twelfth Night* is less love than love-literacy, the book-fed, song-intoxicated mental world of the Petrarchan sonnet, parodying the late Elizabethan love-cult to which Shakespeare himself contributed (and travestied) in his Sonnets.

The world of *Twelfth Night* is textual. But it is textual in the extended sense that courtly and aristocratic life itself, in the dying years of the old queen's reign, super-subtly emulated art, enacting the Spenserian allegories and Platonistic fabrications it had projected on to the page, on a day-to-day basis – imitating the imitation. Organized on an intricately ritualized myth of a virgin sovereign 'served' by court and country as hopelessly worshipping and professedly unworthy lovers, the Court of Elizabeth I was a living embodiment of the sonnet-situation. On certain days, the whole court might wear allegorical white; on others green. As portraits of Elizabeth demonstrate, all her clothes were curious and ornate texts to be read; she was a walking emblem-book, voluminously self-referring, down to her very hairstyle. Masques were put on for Elizabeth, but masque was where she lived, her 'natural' element in a world where nothing was natural but all experience an aesthetic construct. *Twelfth Night* relates, with delicate irony, to Elizabethan decadence, where a book-bound élite had tomes in their bosoms rather than hearts (Viola's exposition of the 'text' and 'chapter of his [Orsino's] bosom' (I.5.215–17)) and where the beloved is only a catalogue of attributes, with no face, only a picture of a face, cosmetically embellished. The great wooing-scene (I.5) in which Viola addresses, implicitly criticizes and involuntarily smashes Orsino's suit to Olivia, is concerned with the *representation* of love rather than with love itself, a parody of the outrageous jargon by which love is conventionally articulated: sacrilegious 'adorations', pumped-out 'fertile tears', eardrum-threatening 'groans that thunder love', red-hot 'sighs of fire' (244–5). In their place, Viola substitutes her own impromptu poem, led credulously by the nose into a sublime act of folly – the artistic revelation of her superior vitality and intelligence – by the leading question, 'Why, what would you?':

> *Make me a willow cabin at your gate,*
> *And call upon my soul within the house;*
> *Write loyal cantons of contemnèd love*
> *And sing them loud even in the dead of night;*
> *Hallow your name to the reverberate hills,*

> *And make the babbling gossip of the air*
> *Cry out 'Olivia!' O, you should not rest*
> *Between the elements of air and earth,*
> *But you should pity me.*

(I.5.257–65)

Viola advertises herself not only as a handy architect (*Make me a willow cabin*) but also as an author (*Write loyal cantons*) and musician (*sing them loud*): a performing artist, scripting her own parts and discharging them too, *con brio*, as she largely does in the play until she – here – hoists herself with her own petard. Far from hanging around under the Lady's balcony, or sending messengers from a safe distance, Viola would dig in and set up camp, forcing an entry by the sheer hullabaloo of her persistence. Shakespeare at once mocks and exploits the Petrarchan tradition: his subversion of the system by humour (not least, the victim's insomnia) is paradoxically its reclamation. *Ars est celare artem*: the poem acts as a quasi-literary 'device' (bearing comparison with the literary forgery which is the 'device' which fools Malvolio). It works upon Olivia through conjuring an imaginative sound-picture of a world in which she would be loved not by book but from the vivid heart. The implicit image of Echo that makes the 'reverberate hills' shout back suggests a resonance that seems to awaken articulate life out of indifferent silence. Emptiness becomes plenitude, which rings Olivia's name from every compass-point. Viola's promise to 'call upon my soul within the house' picks up the Petrarchan conceit of the lost or stolen heart; the Platonist longing for the lost 'other self' which haunts the play and involuntarily suggests to Olivia that Viola/'Cesario' somehow *is* what she lacks and must have. Thus Olivia is fooled, and Viola makes a fool of herself, through her exuberantly natural tendency to act. The counterfeit text, with all its zestful, illusory beauty, is the banana skin on which they both barge headlong into folly: *we three*, perhaps, for the beguiled audience is just as enchanted.

4. On How Sir Andrew Needed a Dictionary but the Fool was a Thesaurus

'Cesario' is a pun in human form: two meanings covered by the same sign, one superficial, the other subliminal. Puns are fleeting threats to the stability of the linguistic order; we like to 'crack' them and lay them aside as trivial for they expose the unsettling ambiguity at the heart of language. Puns are flukes of sound, homophonic freaks. Like identical opposite-sex twins, they connote self-contradictory signification such as that which makes 'Cesario' a catalytic threat to the fixed order 'he' infiltrates. The special intimacy felt by audiences with Viola is partly due to the fact that only we 'get' the pun; she dramatizes a quality of hidden, unreadable meaning, unavailable to her fellow-characters.

Throughout the action sweeps the delirious energy of a momentous play upon words' double meaning, a spree of language carried on by Sir Toby (a domesticated Falstaff), Maria, the Clown and Viola herself. Cunning even in his cups, the lavish epicure of others' verbal folly, Sir Toby stage-manages Sir Andrew's linguistic maladroitness so as to raise inanity to a fine art:

SIR TOBY *Accost, Sir Andrew, accost.*
SIR ANDREW *What's that?*
SIR TOBY *My niece's chambermaid.*
SIR ANDREW *Good Mistress Accost, I desire better acquaintance.*
MARIA *My name is Mary, sir.*
SIR ANDREW *Good Mistress Mary Accost –*
SIR TOBY *You mistake, knight. 'Accost' is front her, board her, woo her, assail her.*
SIR ANDREW *By my troth, I would not undertake her in this company. Is that the meaning of 'accost'?*

(I.3.46–56)

Accost. Where every word represents a slippery problem, the English language is riddlingly open to interpretation. Insecurity as to part of speech comes first: is the unfamiliar term *accost* a proper noun, the unfamiliar woman's name? The booby knight takes a deep breath and plunges in on that assumption. Wrong. Maria corrects him but offers insufficient data and bearings. 'My name is Mary, sir.' Inserting this Christian name before the putative surname, Sir Andrew prepares to relaunch his apostrophe. Wrong again. Sir Toby intervenes with a dictionary definition of *accost*, with a twinkle in his eye. Exploiting the nautical roots of the word (one ship 'going alongside another', berthing with a view to boarding), Sir Toby extracts from the word a series of helpful near-synonyms which, however, take Sir Andrew fatally back to some unhelpful and socially disastrous implications of the original coinage, for 'front', 'board' and 'assail' may carry aggressive sexual connotations. These bawdy innuendoes are recognized by Sir Andrew and misconstrued with gross literality, yielding the shocked punch-line of the sequence: 'I would not undertake her in this company', unconsciously implying that in other company, or none, he might do his best to come aboard, from which protest he desperately shrinks to a direct query as to the meaning of the word. The subject here is less Sir Andrew's relation with Sir Toby or Maria than the comedy of language itself, its volatile susceptibility to incontinent change and absurd misconstruction: especially its capacity to fool and embroil the incompetent user. Language spanks Sir Andrew for fooling with its play of many senses and innuendoes. Now Maria takes over the pumping and trouncing of the victim. 'Fair lady,' bleats Sir Andrew, 'do you think you have fools in hand?' 'Sir, I have not you by the hand' (I.3.61–3). And so it goes on, allowing Maria to establish herself as an expert practitioner in wit in the quintessential game of come-uppance which is a major pastime in Illyria, dealing out the literal among the metaphorical, breeding twin meanings from a single word and making the twin meanings breed again in their turn.

Take away the puns and there is no *Twelfth Night*. Its rich play of subversive fantasy is founded on double meaning, presenting a study in what the able wordmonger' can get away with. Maria, for instance, is 'my niece's chambermaid': not a cleaning-girl, of course, but a household-member higher up the social scale, a woman-in-waiting, who shares Olivia's private life. In her witty altercation with Sir Andrew, she gets away with calling and proving him a fool by a slick succession of insulting metaphors which speed ahead of his addled intelligence ('What's your metaphor?' (68–9)) and never hurt him because he never really knows he's down. At the same time, she sticks to the polite forms of address proper to her inferior status, calling him *you* (as opposed to the intimate, superior or contemptuous *thou*) and, on every single occasion in this dialogue when she addresses him, recognizes his rank as *sir*. Thus, while observing the polite forms which endorse the social order (however ironically she may inflect them), she subverts them through assuming command of the verbal medium, and sustaining that command. Linguistic power is a major factor in social dominance in this play. The agile wit overleaps the bounds of decorum unpunished, while the protagonist of single, uncontaminated and God-given meanings (Malvolio) is caught out by fictions which lure out his own suppressed fantasies. While Maria capitalistically rises (the investment of her wit earns her Sir Toby's hand), Malvolio falls: his pretension to the hand of his employer lands him lower in dignity and esteem in the feudal fixity of the great household than he had been at the beginning of the play.

The nautical metaphor, true to the maritime character of Illyria, resurfaces when Viola, in her role as the 'Duke's gentleman', is confronted by Maria and shown the door at 'Cesario's' first meeting with Olivia:

MARIA   *Will you hoist sail, sir? Here lies your way.*

VIOLA   *No, good swabber, I am to hull here a little longer. Some mollification for your giant, sweet lady!*

(I.5.194–7)

Here one wordmongering idiot-detector meets another, and the best 'man' wins. Viola gets the last word, using the very method by which Maria sunk Sir Andrew in the shallows of his own intellect. At Maria's invitation to clear off (in nautical terms ironically reminiscent of Viola's actual but unknown sea-borne arrival), Viola points out that she is in port on her own terms. *Good swabber* dismisses Maria as a menial deck-hand, Olivia's cleaning-woman. Viola's mannishly swaggering discourse, riding the high horse of her assumed gentleman's prerogative, puts down the 'giant' mite (Maria is evidently envisaged as of minuscule height, 'the youngest wren of nine' (III.2.63) with bravura ease, by pointing out her low social status.

Sir Toby introduced Sir Andrew to Maria (who already knew better) as the complete type of the Renaissance gentleman, a man of culture and a bit of a polyglot, for he 'speaks three or four languages word for word without book, and hath all the gifts of nature' (I.3.24–5). The infamous speciousness of this advertisement is not apparent to the audience until it has seen Sir Andrew and heard him trip at the first obstacle of the word *accost*. The player of the viola da gamba and the humanist scholar of languages is seen to be without an iota or smidgen of the information necessary for the production of a gentleman in Elizabethan England. The educated classes were trained in rhetoric and public-speaking from an early age, learning from tutor or schoolmaster the essential art (not an adornment but an accoutrement of virility and

caste, like the wearing of a sword), the rules of public-speaking: *inventio,
dispositio, elocutio, memoria, pronuntiatio* – the matter, its arrangement,
eloquent expression, memorization and presentation. Poor Sir Andrew:
his mind, as he goes on to regret, has an infantine innocence of such
endowments. His large title sits vacantly on his tiny head like a fool's
cap. The gift of the gab, equated with the gentleman's magnanimity
and authority, and proof not only of human superiority to the animal
kingdom but also of aristocrat to burgher and artisan, is wonderfully
lacking: 'O, had I but followed the arts!' (I.3.90–91). Textbooks were
not lacking on how to acquire these cultural skills, from Castiglione's
The Courtier to Puttenham's *The Arte of English Poesie*, which set
rhetoric out simply so that even ladies might get a smattering. Sir
Andrew, earnestly conscious of his defects in this particular, though
not always of their cavernous profundity, is always on the lookout
for supplementation of his literary and linguistic gifts. His letter-
writing declares him 'a clodpole' (III.4.186) and his epistle will have to
be scrapped, as Sir Toby realizes when stage-managing the duel with
'Cesario' in Act III; but it is certainly not for want of trying. When
Sir Andrew's 'rival' apostrophizes Olivia with the affected circumlocu-
tions and elaborate hyperbole of courtly discourse, Sir Andrew is
much struck, not noticing that 'Cesario's' parodic language artfully
borders on the verge of idiocy, for her mouthfuls of euphuistic hyperbole translate into an invitation to the sky to drop smells on her
auditor:

VIOLA   *Most excellent, accomplished lady, the heavens rain odours
          on you!*
SIR ANDREW *That youth's a rare courtier. 'Rain odours'! Well.*
VIOLA   *My matter hath no voice, lady, but to your own most
          pregnant and vouchsafed ear.*
SIR ANDREW *'Odours'; 'pregnant'; and 'vouchsafed'. I'll get 'em all three
          all ready.*

(III.1.81–88)

For Sir Andrew, the ardent student of linguistic (and hence social, and
matrimonial) eptitude, 'Cesario' is a walking textbook of linguistic
manners, Castiglione's courtier on legs: he notes the youth's fancy
diction for his own future use. His diligent attentiveness to the faculty
he lacks and which Viola possesses, perhaps in excess of her real interests, draws our attention to the rich incongruity of language in the play,
the enchantments of its faking and feigning power, and the wonder of
freshly coined or idiosyncratically applied diction – 'odours', 'pregnant',

'vouchsafed'. These impressive words, with their particular (and ironically specious) lilt and flavour, belong to Viola's individual parlance, which Sir Andrew could no more lift from his rival's personality and graft on to his own than he could saw off the youth's leg and walk on it. This is only one of many recurrent occasions on which *Twelfth Night* reflects upon its own language, reinforcing our awareness that it is a play upon words: like the genie in the tale, its persons are illusions, word-begotten, word-shaped, word-constructed, and must retreat to the inside of the lamp of the text in the end. Language by rote or copied down from the book verbatim is a comic victim of *Twelfth Night*. Malvolio will 'read politic authors' to prepare his squelching of Sir Toby (II.5.155); Viola travesties such language in her book-mocking conning of her speech, which insists on its own artificiality: 'Alas, I took great pains to study it, and 'tis poetical' (I.5.187). Viola's linguistic panache resists imitation because it takes liberties with the rule-bound basis of Renaissance love-rhetoric: a liberty itself prescribed by the book.

Sir Andrew's mental annotations imply his need for a dictionary. Supplied with a compact lexicon of the English language, he might not have shuffled as forlornly along the shoreline of the sea of words. To remind ourselves that no English dictionary existed until 1604, when Robert Cawdrey published one on the model of the Latin dictionaries, is to recall the unfixed, expanding and volatile condition of the English language in this period – a fact that has relevance to the whole corpus of Renaissance English literature, and a specific aptness to *Twelfth Night*, that feast of words. The language was still unstandardized or regulated by appeal to a uniform and consensus systematization. Words, pre-dictionary, were free – freer at least than they have ever been since. Trapped between the covers of a dictionary, language achieves a stasis and an authorized pre-emptive solidity not suffered by words in unclassified circulation. The rules of grammar had been codified in the 1580s by William Bulloker; spelling reform under Bulloker, John Hart and Alexander Gil was catching up on the messy, chaotic variability which hitherto reigned like a Lord of Misrule, allowing words to trespass freely on others, and saturnalian puns and word-play to breed through mismating. However, even spelling standardization had not set hard in Shakespeare's day: he himself could sign his name in a pleasant variety of ways. In the lexis, agreed meanings, spellings and pronunciation had not bred conformity. And further to bewilder Sir Andrew, the period was one of unprecedented linguistic expansion: between 1500 and 1700, the English vocabulary trebled in size, though many words had brief life-spans. Neologism was both a necessity and a fad: there were not enough words to go round. Latin was ransacked for coinages (breeding the famous 'ink-horn' controversy), obsolete Anglo-Saxon root-words (archaism and purism), other European borrowings, as well as affixation, suffixation, compounding and grammatical transference. The language *Twelfth Night* is sounding, therefore, answered to the subtitle of the play, *What you will* – or, perhaps, *What you can get away with.* This comparative freedom, and the liberty to coin new words, made for a richness of the lexis which rhetoricians called *copie*, or copiousness, much prized in a vernacular which was self-consciously rivalling Latin and Norman French for pre-eminence. *Copie* depends on the existence of manifold near-synonyms, each with a peculiar resonance and connotation; it makes for a choiceful vocabulary, with the capacity for vivid surprise. The Shakespearian *copie*, so extravagant in the richly formal poetry of *Romeo and Juliet* and the minefield of verbal excess that is *Hamlet*, is restrained in *Twelfth Night* to the decorums of a form in which emotional effects frequently reside in the saying of too little, and the subtle play of elegant voices, or the vigorous exchange of idiomatic jest and imagistic insult. But the playwright of *Twelfth Night* is always a language-creator as well as a language-user: the molten fluidity of pre-dictionary language is evident even in the restraint and finesse of so tightly composed a play. Nothing is copied out straight from the rule book of comic or romance convention or taken at the dictation of the common average.

When Sir Andrew's admiration was kindled by the flourish of 'Cesario's' fanfare-greeting to Olivia, he was taken by the saying of the expected thing in unpredictable language. In this he showed sagacity, for it is everywhere a powerful element in Shakespeare's style: the saying of a fairly ordinary thing in a fractionally abnormal way, which then leads on to a further slight abnormality – creating a total effect of minute curvature from the straight line, like the bias of a bowl in Sebastian's metaphor (V.1.256–7). To read is to experience a succession of soft shocks, each reinforcing the sense of the flair and freshness of what is said and imagined, making us feel that we are in an anterior, or alternative, world of words, gently and continuously surprising, where we have never been before. A happy example of such subtle linguistic aberration occurs when the Duke is indoctrinating 'Cesario' on 'his' mission to act out Orsino's suit to Olivia. 'Cesario' is characteristically subdued and laconic in 'his' unsure reaction to this proposition: 'I think not so, my lord.'

On How Sir Andrew Needed a Dictionary but the Fool was a Thesaurus

ORSINO   *Dear lad, believe it.*
For they shall yet belie thy happy years
That say thou art a man. Diana's lip
Is not more smooth and rubious. Thy small pipe
Is as the maiden's organ, shrill and sound,
And all is semblative a woman's part.

                                       (I.4.29–34)

Irony here is obvious to the point of blatancy. Viola's disguise is transparent – pretty lips (which the Duke has evidently studied) and treble voice. Nor does the passage present any difficulty in comprehension or interpretation: the play upon ironic role-play could not be more obvious in relation to the boy-actor who is playing a girl pretending to be a boy who is exhorted to act the role of the Duke in a manner amenable to the young woman at the receiving end. *Dear lad* is a colloquial endearment which endorses the affectionate, almost paternal, closeness the Duke feels for his companion. But the description of the girlish boy has a sensuous piquancy beyond the threadbareness of its similes: the goddess's lip is conventionally *ruby* but only 'Cesario's' is *rubious*, a Shakespearian coinage for the occasion, which combines *ruby* with *beauteous* and retrospectively disturbs the imagined texture of *smooth* into alluring life: these are lips one might want to kiss. After (perhaps) imitating 'Cesario's' unbroken voice, Orsino concludes that everything about the youth is '*semblative* a woman's part'. *Semblative* is another Shakespearian coinage, from *semblance*, on the model of the French *semblable*. The effect of the substitution for this familiar-sounding but actually unfamiliar and novel polysyllable for the expected *like*, is to draw attention to the illusion represented by 'Cesario' ('he' is a semblance only) and to the illusion-creating possibilities of language. Orsino is not saying 'you are like a woman' but 'you look like someone acting the role of a woman'. That is, of course, true of the boy-actor but false of the girl-character. Coinage increases awareness of the medium of acting and the medium of language in producing the play of double-meaning – of *semblatives* – which is the source of so much of the audience's delight. If, like Sir Andrew, we are tempted to get out a notebook and scribble down Shakespeare's coinages for use on future occasions, such transplantation may not succeed. As one-off jobs, they may be dreamed up for this single occasion, and live a tenuous life on the very borders of the viable. Uncurrent as yet, such coinages are as acceptably freakish and liminal as that 'poor monster' Viola, transitional between states, 'as a squash is before 'tis a peascod, or a codling when 'tis almost an apple ... in standing water between boy and man' (I.5.152–4), as Malvolio says in an uncharacteristic burst of imagery, mistaking the threshold-state maintained by 'Cesario' for the indeterminacy of adolescence rather than dissimulated gender. Shakespeare's pre-dictionary mind seems to have acted on a thesaurus-principle, throwing up showers of near-synonyms which then begat new chains of words: *Twelfth Night* itself not only relishes but also attentively examines the fertile breeding-ground of language, in which an errant genetic principle is at work spawning ulterior or *semblative* meanings with fantastic virtuosity. In a play of doubles, counterfeits, frauds and forgeries, language itself is the protean currency that is always in doubt.

In the figure of the Clown, who lives by the fruits of his tongue and coins words and false proverbs that he may coin money, language is the wherewithal by which word-breeding doubles money. Feste is a language-enricher at the same time as he is a self-enricher. Sir Andrew is spendthrift of praise of the Fool's virtuosity both in singing, dancing and verbal display:

SIR ANDREW ... *In sooth, thou wast in very gracious fooling last night, when thou spok'st of Pigrogromitus, of the Vapians passing the equinoctial of Queubus. 'Twas very good, i'faith. I sent thee sixpence for thy leman, hadst it?*
FESTE *I did impetticoat thy gratillity ...*

(II.3.20–25)

The Folio reading (printed in the Arden edition) is actually *impeticos*. No one ever did before or after Feste *impeticos* anything: Feste struck the word new-minted out of the verb *impocket*, forged together with the noun *petticoat* in a sliding grammar out of the pocket in the Fool's long coat. A *gratillity* was just as unforthcoming in current English: this is the first recorded usage (out of two) in history – a perversion of *gratuity* which seems to jingle the impeticosed coin, which it earns all over again. Freaks and flukes of language fly loose in the air, as Feste double-deals his mother-tongue, arousing all the homonyms which sleep side-by-side in our minds and have to be left there sound asleep if we want to speak functional and workaday sense. Gratuitous gratillities are the reward of 'gracious fooling' – gratillities that are second cousins to scurrilities and bosom friends of futilities and titillations. The Clown sets up a jingling chain-reaction between the grounds of words, calling up funny echoes and setting off inconsequential new meanings as the foundation of a discourse which competes with the norm. Trespassing across linguistic norms which conservatively endorse the *status quo* (for each repeated usage of consensus formulae deepens the groove of unthinking communal assumption), the Fool's verbal licence guarantees entrance to a radically alternative world of language where each word is made to seem scintillatingly alive and peculiarly interesting in its own right – as diverting as the Fool's bauble, as provocatively critical as his mirror, as queer as the world viewed for the first time, with the protective and muffling felt of common usage peeled off. *Twelfth Night* focuses the extent to which we use language as a comforting upholstery and cushioning which is laid over every unaccommodating surface of reality, so that we can bear to live with it and feel secure there. Agreed language domesticates the world we have to live in and constructs its meaning to our use and comfort. It is fitting that a play set within the domestic interior (and a cultivated garden), and concerning itself with the management of a hierarchically ordered indoor life of art and artifice, should expose the language of order to the scrutiny of such double vision. The Fool, with his wily capitalistic attitude to words and his possession of what amounts to a philosophy of language, is the prime lunatic-detector in the play. The ship of fools carries its universal cargo; vanity and illusion, as he keeps pointing out, are the rule, monopolizing the language and behaviour which constitutes the Illyrian 'norm'.

The insecurity of tenure endured by the Fool, hanging on by the skin of his teeth to a household in which he is a dependant, corresponds to the instability of the language which is his tackle and trade. His marginal status at Olivia's household is made evident from his first entrance, in which Maria warns him that his habit of absconding is wearying Olivia and wearing out his welcome:

MARIA   *Yet you will be hanged for being so long absent; or to be turned away – is not that as good as a hanging to you?*

FESTE   *Many a good hanging prevents a bad marriage; and for turning away, let summer bear it out.*

                                          (I.5.15–19)

The Fool is, strictly speaking, a hanger-on, not a necessity in the ordering of the household like Malvolio (for whom Olivia expresses considerable esteem) but a supernumerary luxury item, kept on for light relief, and a relict of her father's time. Feste shrugs off the consequences of being 'turned away' – becoming a homeless vagrant – hoping for warm weather should the worst come to the worst. But his marginal relation to the community (parallel with Viola/'Cesario's'), which makes his existence tricky and precarious, gives it a certain outsiderly authority. The Fool's gifts are severely Socratic and dialectical when brought to bear on matters of life and death. His first feat is sagaciously to prove, against the grain of her evident irritation, that his mistress's prolonged rites of mourning are based on double-think:

FESTE   *. . . Good madonna, give me leave to prove you a fool.*

OLIVIA   *Can you do it?*

FESTE   *Dexteriously, good madonna.*

OLIVIA   *Make your proof.*

FESTE   *I must catechize you for it, madonna. Good my mouse of virtue, answer me.*

OLIVIA   *Well sir, for want of other idleness, I'll bide your proof.*

FESTE   *Good madonna, why mourn'st thou?*

OLIVIA   *Good fool, for my brother's death.*

FESTE   *I think his soul is in hell, madonna.*

OLIVIA   *I know his soul is in heaven, fool.*

FESTE   *The more fool, madonna, to mourn for your brother's soul, being in heaven. Take away the fool, gentlemen.*

(I.5.52–67)

The parody catechism, in exposing the distance between the consolations of Olivia's professed Christian faith and the apostate implications of her behaviour, reveals a genuine ambiguity in Feste's mistress. He makes her pause for thought and simultaneously take heart. The Fool performs in miniature a rite of passage for Olivia, delivering her from the trauma of lost origins into the period of search for identity and bearings. His service is to lead her across a narrow, precarious bridge between mourning and receptiveness to new life. Under his tutelage, she lays her bereavement to rest and is never the same again. It is often observed by readers that, though Olivia is alleged to be devoted to mourning, this is not evident in her demeanour in the play: but this is surely because the Clown performs a comic exorcism or *katharsis* for her in Act I, a benign office or ministry, ironically suited to his 'priestly' role. As the mock-catechism proceeds, so tension mounts. Symmetrical question and answer bring out real anger and pain in Olivia, who is forced to acknowledge her malaise, by a retainer who balances on a perilous margin between doing her good and giving hurt and offence. The Fool never stands in greater danger of being turned away than when he ventures the unthinkable 'I think his soul is in hell, madonna.' The shock at once arouses and releases tension in Olivia's 'I know his soul is in heaven, fool.' Pouncing upon her in the full flight of her righteous indignation, the Fool seizes advantage by putting up the comic mirror to her ambiguity: a mirror in which she will have no choice but to acknowledge that 'fool' and 'madonna' are one and the same person. This curative wisdom acts by the arousal and dispersal of nervous tension: it is a performance-art, dependent on split-second timing, which treads a fine line between giving tasteless offence (and thus endangering his own licensed position) and offering good but unwanted advice in a form which can be tolerated by the sensitive ego.

Through such shrewd and inventive use of his verbal gifts, the unnecessary Fool creates a sort of *ad hoc* tradesman's entrance for himself in the world of Olivia's household – which entrance Malvolio labours to board up against him. Their mutual and inveterate antagonism is sounded immediately after the catechism: 'I marvel your ladyship takes delight in such a barren rascal . . .' (I.5.78–9). These insults are remembered by Feste until the play's end, and it is their threat not only to his welcome but also to his livelihood that he punishes, again by catechism, in his disguise as Sir Topas in Act IV. Double-talk, double-think, dubiety, paradox, two-facedness are the breeding-ground for his wit and the source of lucre. Play is his work, as it was Shakespeare's, the theatre being a market-place, subject to the whims of audiences and the competition of rivals, in which the actor-playwright had considerable investments and had by 1596 reaped enough profits to build himself a gentlemanly property. Feste is the sophist with words for sale, rate of exchange unspecified. Whatever he can scrounge, he will double. Financial transactions consistently accompany his exchanges: people pay him for his songs, or his jests, or bribe him to go away:

ORSINO *Thou shalt not be the worse for me: there's gold.*
FESTE *But that it would be double-dealing, sir, I would you would make it another . . .*
ORSINO *Well, I will be so much a sinner to be a double-dealer; there's another.*
FESTE Primo, secundo, tertio, *is a good play . . .*

(V.1.26–8; 32–4)

Feste invites the magnanimous Duke to double his gift by soliciting a second gift, through using a pun to pin a double meaning into the word *double-dealing*. Double-dealing in the currency of words (lying and fictions) being his own trade, he looks for an answering licence to supply cash-in-hand. Having succeeded, he makes a bid for a third coin (three times lucky). This equation of language with money is an ancient one: we call words *current*; we *coin*, *counterfeit* or *forge* them. Language and money are consensus tokens and symbols, guaranteeing the presence of real value invisibly but systematically signified by them. Or they are the symbols of symbols, as in paper money which is backed by gold. Counterfeits are backed by nothing – meaningless words or valueless currency. To centre attention on the relationship between language and money is to raise the issue of veracity, stability and value in the sign-system: how far can we rely on language as the medium of exchange? It also raises questions of emotional and physical security: if language consistently subverts and disorientates the literal meanings of the signs it uses, how safe can people feel, without guarantee against deception and illusion?

The slippery ambiguity of language which obsessed Shakespeare throughout his writing life was not only the artist's delight but the philosopher's nightmare in Renaissance England. Bacon in his *Novum Organum* spoke of words as prime misleaders. Struggling for a scientific discourse of clear and unilateral meaning, he came up against the absurd disjunction between language and the things it was intended to represent – words for things which don't exist, no words for things which do, numerous words in common currency which are so polysemous as to signify nothing:

> words absolutely force the understanding, put all things in confusion, and lead men away to idle controversies and subtleties, without number ... definitions themselves consist of words, and words generate words, so that, of necessity, recourse must be had to particular instances ...
>
> (*The 'Novum Organum Scientiarum'*, p. 7)

Bacon's attempt to regulate language into some semblance of analytic and empirical utility was, as he records, frustrated by the intransigent resistance of usage-dominated language to any such interference: if you try, 'words cry out and forbid it'. The personification of words as a mutinous populace which is ungovernably committed to saying what it likes (however mindless and meaningless), rather than what the intelligentsia thinks it ought to say, would make a wonderful description of the saturnalian verbal realm of *What You Will*. For Bacon, language could seem the province of anarchy, from which there was virtually no escape, for we have little alternative to language as the medium for deducing and communicating truth. He gives one example of the fourteen different usages of one word (moisture) which makes for fourteen different kinds of ambiguity, and offers the pregnant (and, for the reader of *Twelfth Night*, luminous) observation that 'The light of the understanding is not a dry or pure light, but drenched in the will and affections' (p. 8). The double-dealing, forked-tongued propensity of human knowledge is understood as a function of the ego and the passions, which souse all percepts in their own transforming and deforming wash of imagination. In other words, we read and interpret in the delusive light of *what we will*. Malvolio's cogitations over the forged letter are not the most foolish but the most ridiculously exposed example of this process of egocentric pre-cognition (or 'reading-in') which infects the population of Illyria. Poring with elephantine slowness over the code 'M.O.A.I.' Malvolio reflects, 'And the end: what should that alphabetical position portend? If I could make that resemble something in me' (II.5.116–117). He does not ask 'What does it mean?' but 'What can I plausibly make it mean?' The Illyrian compulsion to decipher the reading self's reflection in the writing, the mirror-world of Narcissus, is at the heart of their incapacity to read the signs by which meaning is communicated. Minds soaked in the Baconian fantasy-light apply themselves to a reality rich in inscrutably double-dealing words which in turn 'generate words' – a teeming spawn of words which, beginning in ambivalence, detach from their duty to signify 'reality' or 'nature', and discharge themselves in chaotic self-reflexive and self-generating fantasy.

Bacon dramatizes the resistance of language to co-operation with reason by endowing words with a kind of cartoon animation: their violent, compulsive energy pugnaciously 'forces' the mind to live by their laws of illogic, 'cry[ing] out and forbid[ding]' the superimposition of rigid meanings by a communal matrix of problematic interrelation which reinforces their doubleness. *Twelfth Night* also endows language with something of this clamorous insistence on its own nonconformity. At the beginning of Act III, the action pauses to allow Viola and the Clown to indulge in word-play, leading to a conversation about language itself. In this scene two kinds of doubleness confront each other: Viola's pun-like dual gender and the equally visual paradox of the Fool's parti-coloured motley. They open with the question of making a living:

VIOLA   *Save thee, friend, and thy music. Dost thou live by thy tabor?*
FESTE   *No, sir, I live by the church.*

(III.1.1–3)

Wilful misconception draws attention to the equivocation latent in the most ordinary and casual sentence constructions. The ensuing persiflage demonstrates that you have to mind your language because you never know exactly what you might be saying. What you understand to be coming out of your mouth may be quite different from what hits the listener's ear. All is subject to interpretation and construction – 'Misprision in the highest degree!' (I.5.50), that major theme of *Twelfth Night*.

The word under pressure here, *by*, links compatibles (Clown and tabor) or incompatibles (Clown and church, king and beggar) depending upon whether its meaning is taken as *beside* (indicating a propinquity that is gratuitous and contingent) or *by means of* (indicating intrinsic relationship), so that the same grammatical construction can make standard sense or affable nonsense. The tiny details of this episode of backchat relate dramatically to the largest themes of the play: Viola, marginal and dependent, queries the Clown's living. The Clown, houseless himself and wearing out a welcome under the shelter of Olivia's roof, evades the question, giving nothing about himself away, and probably lying. Viola's example of the king who 'lies by a beggar' (8) equates the confounding of linguistic distinction with the inversion of social order. The Clown congratulates her dexterity in his own game:

FESTE   *You have said, sir. To see this age! A sentence is but a cheveril glove to a good wit; how quickly the wrong side may be turned outward!*

VIOLA   *Nay, that's certain. They that dally nicely with words may quickly make them wanton.*

FESTE   *I would therefore my sister had had no name, sir.*

VIOLA   *Why, man?*

FESTE   *Why, sir, her name's a word, and to dally with that word might make my sister wanton. But indeed, words are very rascals, since bonds disgraced them.*

VIOLA   *Thy reason, man?*

FESTE   *Troth, sir, I can yield you none without words, and words are grown so false, I am loath to prove reason with them.*

(III.1.11–24)

Sentence refers to the rhetorical form, *sententia*, a pregnant and conclusive utterance, taking the form of a complete unit of grammar. Feste's comparison of such a form with a 'cheveril glove', supple to the subtle mind, made of a leather so soft and stretchable that it can be peeled inside-out and outside-in in the blinking of an eye, emphasizes not only the ductile, paradoxical and beguiling character of language but also its use as a kind of dress – an outward skin we wear, that can be put on and taken off at will. This reversibility of interchangeable face and inside makes language-manipulation peculiarly the province of the dual-coloured Fool in his motley and the reversible gender of Viola, each costumed in a heterodox way, at variance with the standard of the community, and speaking a knowingly bipartisan language. If a glove is turned inside-out, it undoes itself. But to *undo oneself* is Renaissance cant for a sexual fall. Viola lightly takes up this suggestion. To *dally* with words is to make them *wanton*: words' innate disposition to flightiness is agreeably open to the flippant tongue. The Clown's sudden invention of a sister is another metaphor which comically reinforces our sense of the gap between words and things; names and persons. To make free with a name is not to take liberties with the person designated: handling and tampering with the name of your sister leaves your actual sister *virgo intacta*, language being a self-reflexive code of symbols. But by deliberately confounding the symbol with the symbolized, and then reminding us that the sign and the signified *ought* to stand in stable relationship (our word should be our bond, but isn't) Feste calls all language into question.

Essentially he is conducting in the comic key the same interrogation of linguistic duplicity which the tragedies harrowingly undertake. Language as the insidious costume or cosmetic mask of thought is an obsession of *Hamlet*, written in 1602, within two years of *Twelfth Night*. The techniques of verbal play upon double-meaning of the late comedy are brought in the tragedy to shed a lurid light on a dark and spectral underworld of dubiety. The murderous carnality detected beneath the polite silk-screen of language by the Prince in *Hamlet* subverts all order, including the linguistic order. There is no way to ascertain reality through the corrupted language of the court which mouths its fabricated speech like actors in a play, weaving a nearly seamless structure of lies and evasions:

> POLONIUS   *. . . What do you read, my Lord?*
> HAMLET   *Words, words, words.*
> POLONIUS   *What is the matter, my Lord?*
> HAMLET   *Between who?*
> POLONIUS   *I mean the matter that you read, my lord.*
> HAMLET   *Slanders, sir . . .*
>
> (*Hamlet*, II.2.191–7)

The play on *matter* as *subject matter*, *problem* and *quarrel* displays the language-game in Denmark as an embroilment up to the elbows in evil. Words are eaten out with corrupt usage so that falsehood is the only accepted currency; words are weapons with poisoned tips with which one hopes to outwit the opponent. Words bereft of matter become meaningless lies: to use them at all is to risk becoming implicated. In Illyria, the play upon words is a light fantasy-game, as between intelligent children, to whom only temporary and limited harm can come. Double-meaning generates fictions and jests rather than lies. Pain is tranquillized to a gentle echo, as here when the Clown's invention of a 'sister' with 'no name' picks up the theme of brother-sister loss, recalling Viola's fictional *alter ego* dreamed up only two scenes ago: 'My father had a daughter loved a man –' . . . (II.4.106–8). Unknown to the Clown a sister without a name stands inside-out before him in the person of 'Cesario', a *double entendre* which is lost on him. The rascality of words stands plainly demonstrated before our eyes. The Clown's denial that anything can be known using the defective medium of language (and that nothing can be known without it) has a Baconian resonance, and stands unanswerably as a deeply serious conclusion of the Clown's forensic linguistic experimentations. Later in Act III, scene 1, he defines himself as, not Olivia's fool, 'but her corrupter of words' (34–5) – the late-sixteenth-century comic antidote to the optimistic humanist assumption that 'bi language and by eloquence / A man is taught in vertu to be stable' (Lydgate, *The Fall of Princes*). Mastery of eloquence teaches the insecure protagonists how to keep precariously afloat on the unstable welter of linguistic excess: nothing more.

Feste's professed dislike of, or absence of liking for, Viola ('I do not care for you' (28)) is a gratuitous little extra detail adding curious bite to the exchange. But indeed, the Clown does not, properly speaking, like anyone. The stage fool is No One, or hardly anyone. He will play with you, or against you, sending you up as a mirror makes a scarecrow of the casual observer. His stock-in-trade is muted aggression, bred of a judicious and democratizing distaste for human nature. Dealing in craftily audacious digs and pinches, he needles his victims on their sorer points: the youth's beardless chin, for instance; 'his' role as pander between Olivia and Orsino (43–4; 50–51). Leaving 'Cesario', he promises to announce to his employers an unknown visitor on unknown business using an unknowable medium:

I will conster to them whence you come. Who you are and what you would are out of my welkin – I might say 'element', but the word is overworn.

(III.1.55–7)

To conster means to construe or interpret. How impossible this is in the mesmerizing play of Illyrian identities and mist of cloudy words, the Fool thinks he knows. The audience knows he does not know all. He is, for instance, ignorant of 'whence ['Cesario'] comes', which is the only aspect of 'Cesario' he thinks he can feel sure about. On the riddle of 'who you are' and 'what you would' he maintains a firm position of Socratic ignorance: a condition of unique wisdom which naturally requires outlandish expression. The outworn word *element* (over-used in the Jonsonian 'humours' comedies) gives way to *welkin*, a word which does not fit. In a language where all signs are questionable by the impartial user, one might meaningfully say anything, or nothing, or everything. When Viola and Feste confront one another, it is as if two mirrors view one another, seeing – nothing at all. Viola, the indeterminate mirror which reflects whatever the wistfully self-deluding observer puts in it, encounters an indeterminate, illusionless double in the Fool, equally polysemous and without desires of his own to project upon his companion (except the need for ready cash).

Feste's most characteristic rhetorical figure is that of anti-metabole, in which sentence-elements are glibly reversed; he transforms sense into a kind of mirror-writing, right-to-left rather than left-to-right, where the elements are stable but reversal destabilizes their meaning. His other linguistic tools are tautology ('for what is "that" but "that"? And "is" but "is"?' (IV.2.15–16)) and paradox ('Nothing that is so, is so' (IV.1.8)). In *Twelfth Night* much of what is said is confusing, misconstrued or downright incomprehensible to the listener. The play artfully dramatizes a gap between the speaker's mouth and the listener's ear, a state of affairs triggered by the threefold trick (Viola's disguise and the emergence of the boy-twin; the joke played on Malvolio; the duel) but also commensurate with experiences familiar in everyday life: the feeling that we imperfectly understand people's motives, behaviour and language: that others are 'faces' only, masking unguessable hidden strangers; the masquerade of costume, class and social role; tangential speech expresses obliquely what is felt as unsafe to admit. Not only roles but language itself may, activated by a state of passion or delusion, seem to speak through one, as if ventriloquially 'possessed', a comic motif of the play which links Olivia's compulsive love-talk with Malvolio's incomprehensible outbursts in Act III. The question of identity lies at the root of the double-talk in which all the characters at some time participate. Taken up by 'fancy' (connoting either 'imagination' or 'love'), protagonists enter a transforming, protean area in which the boundaries of the self are threatened and suffer temporary dissolution: in this vertiginous space, the persons in the play both *are* and *are not* themselves. Shakespeare invents and weaves variations on a language to express this instability by focusing on an instability already present in language itself:

> OLIVIA *Stay.*
> *I prithee, tell me what thou think'st of me?*
> VIOLA *That you do think you are not what you are.*

> OLIVIA   *If I think so, I think the same of you.*
> VIOLA   *Then think you right; I am not what I am.*
> OLIVIA   *I would you were as I would have you be.*
> VIOLA   *Would it be better, madam, than I am?*
> *I wish it might, for now I am your fool.*
>
> (III.1.134–41)

In this exchange of symmetrical antithesis, riddle retaliates upon riddle, using the rhetorical device of stichomythia, a formality at variance with the more naturalistic flow of *Twelfth Night* which therefore draws attention to its own technical stylization, as the fencers duel with a language which struggles in a mesh of ambivalent meanings. Laingian 'knots' cryptically subject key-terms to a frenzy of repetition: *think* occurs five times; the verb *to be* seven; *I* and *me* eleven; *you* and *thou* ten. This mounting frenzy excludes almost any words save those at issue, which it renders progressively less intelligible through wrestling repetition. Shakespeare concentrates the whole play's ironies in this rhetorical display, which only Viola and (with difficulty) the audience can fully understand. Viola thinks that Olivia thinks that she is in love with a man; Olivia thinks that Viola thinks she is not in love with a woman; Viola thinks Olivia is right to think she (Viola) is not what she pretends to be – *I am not what I am*; Olivia wishes Viola would be as she (Olivia) desires. Thus the chain of cross-purposes depends upon the particularities of plot in this one play. But it also reflects a potentiality for undermining identity resident in language all the time, the latent power of the sign-system (which depends on difference to maintain meaning and order) to collapse distinction. For after all, to me, I am 'I' and you are 'you', but to you, you are 'I' and I am 'you'. Identities easily become indistinguishable because we use the same terms to differentiate them. The audience laughs to testify to its delight at the cleverness of the skirmish, but even so there is a lonely sadness at the heart of the riddle, a separateness of speaker from speaker, a separation-anxiety which haunts the play and is generated by the fact that, failing a miracle, such as a boy-twin waiting in the wings, fallible words are all we have by which to know one another.

In the theatre, such poignant reflections – midway between *Träumerei* and trauma – are never permitted long lease of life. Close on the scene of Viola's and Olivia's riddling entanglement comes an outrageous discharge of linguistic energy as that dormouse, Sir Andrew (III.2.18), is called to arms. Imagery and conceit teem and breed in the mouths of the conspirators who, through global magnification of the minuscule and reduction of human scale to the measure of a flea's foot (60), manifest the power of comic creativity to collapse the boundaries of the world in which we live and to found colonies in the uncharted world of absurdity beyond norms. Imaginative language performs dilations and shrinkages that release the audience's joyous recognition of a surreal cartography which discovers a New World in the virgin territory of the good joke:

FABIAN ... *you are now sailed into the north of my lady's opinion; where you will hang like an icicle on a Dutchman's beard ...*

(24–6)

SIR TOBY ... *If thou 'thou'-est him some thrice it shall not be amiss, and as many lies as will lie in thy sheet of paper – although the sheet were big enough for the bed of Ware in England, set 'em down ...*

(42–6)

MARIA ... *He does smile his face into more lines than is in the new map with the augmentation of the Indies. You have not seen such a thing as 'tis.*

(74–6)

First Sir Andrew endures a process of transportation, diminution and freezing into an icicle on the beard of the Dutch explorer William Barentz rounding Nova Zembla in 1596–7, to emerge into the Arctic of Olivia's distaste; then his writing-paper expands to a sheet on the vastly hospitable bed of Ware (nearly eleven foot square) overseas 'in England'; finally Malvolio's face wrinkles up in paroxysms of smiling into the new map of 1599 with its radiating rhumb-lines. A proto-Metaphysical wit consists not only in wild expansions of perspective but also in the inclusion of vivid and topical but utterly superfluous detail; indeed, the more gratuitous and extraneous the imagery, the deeper is our pleasure. The far-fetched is also far-reaching, and navigates a map always in the making in a comic world never fully known or explored, for, as Maria predicts, *You have not seen such a thing as 'tis.* The writing comes down to us still warm from the pen, with the immediacy of the creative moment alive in its characters.

5. Textual Strategy: Malvolio, the Puritans and the Audience

In his copy of the Shakespeare Folio, King Charles I inscribed 'Malvolio' beside the title of *Twelfth Night* in the contents list. For him, perhaps, as for many audiences, Olivia's steward *was* the play, in gratitude for the aching *katharsis* of the laughter he releases. The wide-openness to interpretation which gives Shakespearian drama its perpetual freshness is nowhere more fully observable than in the radically diverse readings generated by Malvolio's character – from the 'richness and dignity ... a sort of greatness' of Bensley's late-eighteenth-century performance recorded in Charles Lamb's account of 1823 (in Palmer, p. 40), to the farcical figure in the Royal Shakespeare Company's production of 1966, with a headful of curlers under a long white knitted nightcap. Reactions to the baiting of Malvolio in Act IV have also been polarized: he is the killjoy who got what was coming to him or a pitiable figure, as 'notoriously abused' as he claims to be, whose rough treatment in the dark room is grotesquely disproportionate to his offence against the comic norms.

Malvolio's career opens in the latter stages of Act I, when he is revealed as rancorously opposed to the Clown and we begin to see how he will live up to his name (MAL plus VOLIO, 'bad will' – or, better, since he requires a cure, 'ill will' – the antithesis of the subtitle, *What You Will*) by opposing the jest and frivolity represented by Feste (I.5.70 ff.). In the course of this scene, he is seen running errands between Olivia and Viola, and again in Act I, scene 2. In the great 'cakes and ale' scene, Malvolio seeks to suppress the late-night party of Sir Toby, Sir Andrew, Feste and Maria, and incurs the displeasure of the comedy; at the climax of this Act he is viewed from behind a box-tree fantasizing over a liaison with Olivia and taking the bait of the forged letter (II.5); in the show-stopping Act III, he appears in his yellow stockings, cross-gartered and villainously smiling, at the height of his delusion, to be baited by the conspirators; Act IV is the crisis of the Malvolio plot, in which he is constrained in the darkened room and treated as a lunatic; in Act V he reappears, sore and enraged, to end the play on a note of sour disharmony. Thus the Malvolio action unfolds throughout the whole drama, interweaving with the two other actions (Viola/Olivia/Orsino, Sebastian/Antonio), and providing recurrent vital contrast. The role is exclusively a prose part – save for the dignified rhetoric of the poetry to which he rises as he puts his case in Act V – a freely flowing prose, wonderful for its snooty officiousness, the profound seriousness with which it takes itself, its unself-knowing egotism and the bubbling, childish vitality of the fantasy which comes welling up when the lid of propriety is removed. Malvolio's is, in fact, a character of singular complexity and nuance: the play insists on a subtle sense of living personality, earnest, repressed, able to be hurt, arrogant because it is socially uncertain, and speaking officialese as a cover for the desires it scrupulously avoids acknowledging. To play Malvolio as a buffoon is to falsify the system of verbal hints Shakespeare lays down to a character who, ever spuriously on his dignity, yet does have a dignity, to which the folly into which he falls offers a wildly but sadly funny contrast. To simplify Malvolio into the low comic convention of the 'stage steward' or 'stage Puritan' is again a falsification. Such elements are present only as aspects of as profound a study in human nature as Shakespeare ever created – as profound in its way as Lear or Hamlet. For Lear too was a species of cross-gartered gull in a world which mocked him; he stretched out his hands for the ego-comfort of a merely nominal crown as Malvolio kept fingering his chain of stewardly office; like Malvolio, Lear was the fool of his play, cast out to the wasteland and the wolves as the penalty for his folly, as Malvolio is thrown to the dogs of comic retribution. Malvolio is to comedy what Lear is to tragedy: the sacrifice and scapegoat. But while tragedy demands blood, the atoning figure in comedy is nailed on laughter. Laughter is the lash with which the killjoy who spurns the fun is dealt a punitive blow to the only part of his moral anatomy which is soft, sentient and exposed: his pride. However, *Twelfth Night* is not content to yield up the comic victim to the audience as a free gift: the comedy extends its intelligence to incorporate a study of comedy itself. While it builds and releases comic tension in resurgent bouts of laughter, it constrains us to consider the nature and quality of the laughter we collude in emitting, for some laughter is cruel, some embarrassed, and some disturbingly recoils against us from its victim. Just as the language of *Twelfth Night* considers and criticizes language itself, and its aestheticism self-consciously reflects upon itself as an art-work, so its comedy tests laughter and both exploits and explores us, the laughers.

Charles I's copy of the Folio, which placed the mnemonic 'Malvolio' beside the title, reminds us of a preference, but also, no doubt, of a literary revenge upon a very present thorn in the Stuart king's side. For King Charles I in the 1630s and 1640s, a few decades on from

Twelfth Night, lived surrounded by Malvolios, or at least by persons to whom (as it seemed to him) such a temperament, ambition and manners were by no means alien. The disorders of *Twelfth Night* have been felicitously linked with the festively rampant misbehaviour of Elizabethan seasonal holidays. But, arguing with the superior advantages of hindsight, it is also possible to view the drama as a comic mirror applied to the historically real and clamorous social tensions and disruptions whose explosive energies were being felt throughout the late Elizabethan and Jacobean period and would climax in the Puritan Revolution which toppled Charles I and established England as a brief Commonwealth only decades after the writing of *Twelfth Night.* In this reading, 'Count' Malvolio prefigures 'King' Cromwell. The play reflects the social volatility of late Elizabethan England, its class-conflicts, the aspirations of the bourgeoisie, the profligate idleness of the aristocracy and the feudal and hierarchic fixity of an archaic class-system whose boundaries (together with the linguistic boundaries which enshrine and consolidate them) were being threatened by the new economic order of capitalism. The light of comedy refracts and transforms all to laughter: nevertheless that laughter, like every human activity implying a judgement, has a political edge, confirming or challenging a political norm, however blessedly oblivious one may be to this in the pleasure of the moment, as a member of the audience. We laughers are a manipulated mob. Indeed, we have come to the theatre seeking such manipulation – to have our feelings played upon and our sense of humour tickled. In order to document the play's socio-political themes and attitudes, that is, to anatomize out its textual strategies, it may be necessary temporarily to kill the joy of the play, taking what amounts to a Malvolio's-eye view. Modern reader-oriented literary theory opens out a space for such a spoilsport perspective askance from the comic strategy, in order to get an angle on what constitutes the politics of the drama and how its manner manipulates audience-response.

The dramatist either is or hopes to be hand in glove with the audience, winning it over if it does not already share his perspective. *Twelfth Night* is partly structured as a reverse morality play, in which the amoral elements expel the moralistic element, condemning him to a kind of comic hell or purgatory in the process. Shakespeare could assume that the theatre-going public would take little persuasion to join in the ridicule of Malvolio, since from the outset he stands against the spirit of comedy that had attracted it to the theatre in the first place. The very act of attendance distinguished this crowd from that vocal section of the community who objected to plays, players and theatres on sober, godly and orderly – in other words, Malvolian – grounds. The Puritan objection to plays stigmatized theatres as places of profanity, bawdry, theft, prostitution, sodomy, filthy Italianness, wheeler-dealing, sensuality, lies. Stephen Gosson's *The Confutation of Plays* reflected that:

Comedies so tickle our senses with a pleasanter vein, that they make us lovers of laughter, and pleasure, without any mean, both foes to temperance, what schooling is this?

(Hazlitt, W. C., *The English Drama and Stage*, pp. 206–7)

To take moral objection to laughter as involving temporary loss of self-control and hence the danger of a kind of possession or 'ravishing' by the delights of the flesh is an extreme version of the temperance for which Malvolio stands when he condemns the 'uncivil rule' of the revels in Act II (3.119). The comic punishment for the repression of laughter is to be forced to smile, and smile, jaw-cracking smiles, and to be costumed and primed like a buffoon in a play which is scripted all for laughs. The Puritan fright at having one's senses 'tickled' which Gosson hysterically presents in his *Confutation* seems nervously present in Shakespeare's Malvolio too, with his libido held like a tight spring beneath his conscious control, where it vehemently yearns to find an outlet not illicit. This pathological state of sanctimonious smilelessness is presented in *Twelfth Night* as a condition which needs to be brought to the proper surgery for urgent therapy, whether theatre, pub or party:

SIR TOBY   *Out o'tune, sir, ye lie. Art any more than a steward? Dost thou think, because thou art virtuous, there shall be no more cakes and ale?*
FESTE   *Yes, by Saint Anne, and ginger shall be hot i'the mouth too.*

(II.3.110–14)

Two languages have come into explosive collision, Malvolio's insistence on the temperate respect for due 'time' – night being proper for sleep in a civilized household – and Sir Toby's arrogation of 'time' to musical (festive) 'time', measured by the beat of the song they are thundering out. He draws attention, with contumely, to Malvolio's social inferiority, pointing out that the righteous steward can neurotically stint his own palate if he likes but is in no position to ration others. Cakes, ale and spicy (aphrodisiac) ginger are abundantly available to those who want to enjoy themselves.

This memorable 'cakes and ale' speech solicits and easily gets the complicity of the audience with the revellers against Malvolio's puritanical intrusion. This audience, after all, is the one which is taking time off, enjoying a holiday from workaday pursuits, a pastime deplored by the anonymous Puritan author of *A Short Treatise Against Stage-Plays* as 'loss of precious time which should be spent in God's service by those that are hired to be diligent labourers in his vineyard and not be wickedly misspent in such sinful sports' (in Hazlitt, p. 245). Laughter frivolously wastes time which should be dedicated to toil under the eye of the great Taskmaster. The Puritan work-ethic, with its labour-intensive, capital-investment scheme, sees man not as *homo ludens* (the players of games, roles and dramas) but as *homo laborans*, engaged to work the land – and the ploughland of the soul – thriftily for profit, in the name of God's glory. In *Twelfth Night*, no one but Malvolio does a stroke of work from dawn to dusk; all but one are off-duty, even the lady's maid. Time is pastime. The actors in the comedy are working, but then they are working at playing in a comedy that suggests that life can be a comedy: a message no audience needs much encouragement to accept. Viola, of course, marches to and fro on her missions and the Fool may be said to 'work', but not hard – lightly. His business, like that of the actors, is playing, and besides he goes missing when he feels like it; his music-making, he asserts, is done for pleasure. The play equates life and appetite.

The audience, players and dramatist, therefore, whisper among themselves in inveterate conspiracy. Their interest is one. The ideology which they reaffirm by gathering for the particular play is anti-Puritan. Such conspiracy is endorsed by the common satiric attack made on Puritans by Elizabethan and Jacobean drama, from Middleton's *Chaste Maid in Cheapside* to Ben Jonson's Ananias and Tribulation Wholesome in *The Alchemist*. The latter's Zeal-of-the-Land Busy in *Bartholomew Fair*, incensed by the 'heathenish idol[s] ... stage-players, rimers and morrice-dancers' (V.v.5, 10–11) is confuted in theology by a puppet and suffers conversion to profanity; Middleton's Oliver in *The Mayor of Quinborough* suffers the trauma of poetic justice by being forced to view a play:

> For rebels there are many deaths; but sure the only way
> To execute a puritan, is seeing of a play.
> O I shall swound!

> (V.i.190–92)

To make a Puritan see a play is the way drama exacts the death penalty; laughter kills the killjoy. The psychological truth of this perception is demonstrated by the great and secret pain anyone may suffer when exposed to wounding mockery, especially from a taunting crowd. The fundamental aggressiveness is only obscured, not sheathed, by the apparent harmlessness of the form it takes. The anti-Puritan satire of this period releases an artillery-fire of invective in a literary civil war which prefigures the Cavalier–Puritan conflict of the mid seventeenth century. For the Puritan stereotype combines po-faced rigour not only with hypocrisy but also with the character of a rebel. Though in no sense stereotypical, Malvolio's characterization combines such strands. Presenting himself as a solid pillar and bulwark of the existing social order, he is revealed as harbouring anarchic aspirations. His ebullition of fantasy releases an arrant social climber eager to scale the social ladder to its empyrean. He is a respected burgher with high ambitions, ridiculed by the conservative bias of the play, so that the punishment meted out to him is a conservative endorsement of the *status quo*. As a mutinous upstart (gentleman but bourgeois) Malvolio is soundly squelched by the aristocracy, its hangers-on and executive, trounced for his implicit subversiveness and libertinism. Thus a play which initially seems to ridicule the defunct social order (a pusillanimous Duke; a Countess who can't control her household; her uncle and his imbecile pal creating mayhem downstairs) turns out to be permissive of these apparently licentious elements but damning to the ambitions of the law-abiding social climber. 'I'll be revenged on the whole pack of you!' (V.1.375), shouted Malvolio as he slammed out of the play's happy ending: he did just that, in the Civil War of 1642.

But Malvolio is no 'stage Puritan': his profoundly human life comprehends a gamut of qualities from the sterling to the appalling. Sourness and spleen towards Feste in Act I coexist with a real sense of responsibility and duty to Olivia and to the control of the seething cauldron of her household ('Here, madam, at your service', 'Madam, I will' (I.5.289; 297)) and with the childish hauteur with which in his delusion he scorns the flocking little people ('Yes; nightingales answer daws' (III.4.34–5)), as well as his royal answers to the Clown's mad catechism ('I think nobly of the soul . . .' (IV.2.54)). All these qualities endear him to an audience with a kind of awful fellow-feeling. While it is true that I may not have been meant to be Prince Hamlet, I do know something of how it feels to be Malvolio. The stereotypical Puritan lampooned by the Renaissance dramatists was a 'humours' character whose nature was invariable and predictable: a compound of hypocrisy, rant, cant, pride, self-indulgence (including alcohol or roast pork, whichever was on offer), lust and cupidity. He was a big bag of sins of the flesh, just like the rest of us, but worse than the rest of us because he hid his profanity behind a veneer of public piety and unctuous jargon. This is not Malvolio. It is often pointed out that Shakespeare goes out of his way to deny that Malvolio is a Puritan:

SIR TOBY   *Possess us, possess us, tell us something of him.*
MARIA   *Marry, sir, sometimes he is a kind of puritan –*
SIR ANDREW   *Oh, if I thought that, I'd beat him like a dog.*
SIR TOBY   *What, for being a puritan? Thy exquisite reason, dear knight?*
SIR ANDREW   *I have no exquisite reason for't, but I have reason good enough.*
MARIA   *The devil a puritan that he is, or anything, constantly, but a time-pleaser, an affectioned ass that cons state without book and utters it by great swathes; the best persuaded of himself, so crammed, as he thinks, with excellencies, that it is his grounds of faith that all that look on him love him – and on that vice in him will my revenge find notable cause to work.*

(II.3.133–46)

But to go out of one's way to deny that Malvolio is a Puritan is to take the roundabout trouble to call in to the play's frame of reference the idea of a Puritan, all he stands for, and the popular prejudice that the audience brings to the theatre. The issue of Malvolio's Puritanism is problematized from its first mention, for Maria first introduces him as a qualified specimen of the genus ('a kind of puritan') to which our natural query as to *what* kind of Puritan is interrupted and sabotaged by Sir Andrew's expostulation against Puritans and his desire to beat this one up. The short deviation encouraged by Sir Toby's inquiry into exquisite reasons reinforces our already plentiful acquaintance with the vacuity of Sir Andrew's brain and does little to whip up audience prejudice against the godly. But now Maria – presumably upon reflection – has a change of mind: 'The devil a puritan that he is, or anything, constantly . . .', the casual slangy form of which neatly juxtaposes 'devil' and 'puritan' so as to make them seem interchangeable, but seems to detach Malvolio from the very label she initially conferred. The remainder of her speech goes some way towards explaining this. It is vivid, witty, bristling with personal animus. Malvolio's 'grounds of faith', in her book, pertain to no consistent sect or faction but swear allegiance to that sect of one which constitutes the ego – the Great I AM. Maria's caustic and belittling portrait of jumped-up, time-serving pretension – a ridiculous posturer who (like Sir Andrew) stuffs himself with high and mighty expressions learnt by heart which he bestows liberally on all comers ('in great swathes') – is generally read as an adequate diagnosis of Malvolio's condition, especially as it seems confirmed by Olivia's initial condemnation of his lack-laughter absence of proportion ('O, you are sick of self-love, Malvolio . . .' (I.5.85)) and by the subsequent events which demonstrate exactly the susceptibility to flattery she describes. Shakespeare could well have presented this diagnosis without bringing in Puritanism at all; the unresolved confusion he generates over the word's authenticity is a complex way of harnessing the audience's prejudice while avoiding commitment to a polemical stereotype, together with the constraints such a convention would impose on characterization by alienating audience sympathy from a simplified personification: an allegory on stilts. Malvolio, on the contrary, is an inimitable imitation of a person on stilts.

Equally, there is always the possibility that Maria (however successful her experimental hypothesis) might not be quite right. For Malvolio is not presented as an outright 'ass'. Olivia respects and sets store by him: 'Let some of my people have a special care of him. I would not have him miscarry for the half of my dowry' (III.4.62–4), and the Duke is solicitous at the end (V.1.377). In an unruly household, there has always been one dependable retainer. Charles Lamb expressed a perception of this value in the cold dignity of the character:

> Maria describes him as a sort of Puritan; and he might have worn his chain with honour in one of our old roundhead families, in the service of a Lambert or a Lady Fairfax. But his morality and his manners are misplaced in Illyria.
>
> (in Palmer, p. 39)

Writing two hundred years after *Twelfth Night* and nearly a century and a half after the English Civil War and Interregnum, Lamb's thoughts as he casts around for analogies inexorably return to the Puritan Revolution in which the eminent Puritan families governed households grand but not opulent, sternly noble without grandiose display. He returns to a period which Shakespeare did not live to see but the conditions for which he either consciously or unconsciously predicted. Misplaced in Illyria, such an honourable, sober-sided gentleman as Malvolio would be equally misplaced among Cavaliers or at the theatre. (Indeed the Puritans closed the theatres in 1642; expatriate Cavaliers watched neo-classical plays at the Paris court. Malvolio's spoilsport sons and grandsons had their revenge in killing the English drama stone-dead.) Lamb's esteem for Malvolio represents the extent to which, as 'a kind of puritan', the character escapes prejudicial stereotyping of the sort which invites an audience to pelt it with the rotten eggs of their contemptuous laughter, while retaining a recognizable essence of a socially authentic phenomenon.

Malvolio succinctly but subtly represents major Puritan features as authentic aspects of his personality, thought-processes and social behaviour. He is an educated bourgeois to his fingertips, who is at earnest pains to assert himself as a gentleman – presumably because he is acutely aware of his anomalous and tenuous class-position. As a 'steward' he rules the servants but only as the menial executive of the patrician family which lords it over him. Pillar of rectitude though he is, Malvolio shows from his first entrance a characteristic middle-class envy of the authority he is committed to upholding: scratch a Puritan and you find a rebel. It is Malvolio rather than the conspirators who is the true subversive, whom the play's collusive and largely conservative laughter encourages us to put down. The Puritan–capitalist pattern of aspiration, familiar in the history of the period, is reproduced by Shakespeare with detailed insight. Malvolio is also detectably a Calvinist. This aspect of his psychology is elegantly displaced by the substitution of the classical 'Jove' for 'God', a variation which has been assumed to be an emendation of the original text to comply with the 1606 statute forbidding profanity in drama. However, as 'God' appears elsewhere in the play, as well as in other Shakespearian plays of the period, this seems unlikely. My own guess is that Malvolio's commerce with 'Jove' reflects the playwright's desire to inscribe but obscure the Calvinism of the role, endowing it with a larger human resonance than that of the stereotypical Puritan with his jargon of predestined election and reprobation. Malvolio's openness to comic temptation comes partly because he already believes himself to be one of God's chosen 'elect', the saints who shall inherit the earth and trample the profane down to the base of the social heap. Like any Calvinist, he is constantly reading daily life for signs of a providential role: the letter that by miraculous accident comes his way is therefore just one of the evidences and testimonies which common mortals would take for a fluke but which to a Calvinist betokens God's manifest destiny, according to which he must plot his course. It must be stressed that Malvolio's character is by no means reducible to this pattern: the pattern is transfigured into the comic resplendence into which Shakespeare assumes his personality.

In a play of paradoxes, the tension between Malvolio's stewardly fidelity to Olivia and the good conduct of her affairs – his upholding of the *status quo* – and his implicit and subliminal threat to this stability is a paradox maintained from his first entrance. His outspoken disgust with the Clown (his 'inferior') involves him in a covert attack on Olivia (his 'superior') for indulging and maintaining him. Indeed, his first speech to his mistress is so censorious in criticizing her to her face that it borders on insolence:

I marvel your ladyship takes delight in such a barren rascal. I saw him put down the other day with an ordinary fool that has no more brain than a stone. Look you now, he's out of his guard already; unless you laugh and minister occasion to him, he is gagged. I protest I take these wise men, that crow so at these set kind of fools, no better than the fools' zanies.

(I.5.78–84)

This high-handed admonition takes in not only fools but those who indulge and court them: it provokes an immediate retaliation in the diagnostic asperity of Olivia's 'you are sick of self-love, Malvolio . . .' (85). His employer insinuates that it is not consonant with the behaviour of a gentleman ('generous, guiltless, and of free disposition' (86–7), qualities associated with the magnanimity of good breeding) to ascribe disproportionate weight to light-hearted mirth, ignoring the conventions within which it freely functions. Both offended speakers snap at one another fairly sharply in this important (because expository) exchange. Malvolio either does not deign or dare to reply; the Clown gloats. Malvolio's high-handedness operates only just on the hither side of discourtesy. The habits of speech which come through the opening manoeuvres – the formalized superciliousness of 'I marvel your ladyship . . .', and then the pontificating casualness of 'I protest . . .' – are tactics which seek to exert pressure *de haut en bas*. The idiom represents a man overreaching his position, setting right his Lady – a mere young lady – by presenting a perspective more judiciously worldly-wise than she can command. Trading patriarchally on both maleness and seniority, he lets her know that the market value of the fool she keeps is dirt cheap, even as such commodities go. The contempt expressed for the 'wise men' who encourage licensed fools, as being 'no better than the fools' zanies' is scarcely polite, since it mocks the upper classes for self-debasement to mere idiots. In this brief exchange, both Malvolio and Olivia hit hard, where it hurts. Whereas his unspoken implication is that she is unfit for high position and badly in need of his tutelage, hers is that no true gentleman would so distort his judgement.

Class antipathies and the subtleties of class conflict remain a major subject of the play. In Act II, Malvolio is got out of bed to deal with the drunken stridor of Sir Toby, Sir Andrew and the Clown, who on the face of it are confounding all social decorum, starting with time of day ('Not to be abed after midnight, is to be up betimes' (3.1–2)) and extending to the prodigious consumption of alcohol, the proving of knights 'knaves' (63) and word-play of a very mad and bad sort. Maria's entrance to warn of Malvolio's coming ('What a caterwauling do you keep here!' (70)) prepares the way for the righteous irruption of the steward into the proceedings. Sir Toby is cavalier about his niece's displeasure, cocking a drunken snook at her authority by presuming lustily upon pedigree: 'Am not I consanguineous? Am I not of her blood? Tilly-vally! "Lady"!' (76–7). Aristocratic and male licence privileges Sir Toby (in his own estimation) over any mere 'Lady's' propriety, whether or not one is sponging on her hospitality in company with a pedigreed ninny and a plebeian fool. Just as Sir Toby begins to bellow out the song of the play's title, 'O' the twelfth day of December', Malvolio discharges a volley of five indignant rhetorical questions:

My masters, are you mad? Or what are you? Have you no wit, manners, nor honesty, but to gabble like tinkers at this time of night? Do ye make an ale-house of my lady's house, that ye squeak out your coziers' catches without any mitigation or remorse of voice? Is there no respect of place, persons, nor time in you?

(II.3.85–91)

The steward's false position (the duty of remonstrating with his social superiors) is transcended by his evidently ireful glee at being duty-bound to unburden his suppressed resentment and spleen in the form of righteous indignation. To have 'masters' who are manifesting as 'mad' is not to have natural masters. The class system implodes upon its own self-contradictions. Olivia's auxiliary is able to appear to uphold the hierarchy and yet to attack its very foundations. Objecting to the revellers' betrayal of their class obligations by importing into a gracious residence the habits of low-class tradesmen like tinkers and cobblers, proper to a common pub, Malvolio upholds the *status quo*, addressing his 'masters' by the deferential 'you'. At the same time he is empowered to abuse his base 'betters', erecting himself over them as a model of propriety. As Sir Toby and the Clown continue their saturnalian revelry, Maria also remonstrates. Malvolio's cold retorts are succinctly and scathingly offended: 'Is't even so!' (102); 'This is much credit to you!' (105). Indeed Sir Toby has Malvolio at a profound disadvantage, which he snarlingly exploits when he rounds on him: 'Art any more than a steward?' (110–11). The aristocracy is licensed to play the fool, obedient only to the

dictate of *what you will*. When Olivia's subordinate brings in the imperative of *what you ought and must*, his message is humiliatingly derided
not only by Sir Toby's pulling of rank but also by the laughter generated
in the audience by the comedy itself. There is strength in numbers:
Malvolio, always a profoundly isolated figure on the stage, has to bear
the persecution of a minority by the majority. Festive comedy, as a
communal sharing of humour and enjoyment, closes ranks against the
upstart intruder, who dares to protest that it's no joke to be kept awake
at night by other people's noise.

Hence, the audience's laughter upholds the *status quo* against the
party-pooper; liberating comedy against puritanical duty; knightly
licence against middle-class respectability. But here we might pause to
consider whether, if we have ever been tormented by other people's all-
night parties, taunted with low estate or made to feel isolated and
humiliated in a public place, we are not inclined to pity and respect
Malvolio: such rueful fellow-feeling seems to me far easier for readers
than for audience. Seeing his point of view would mean having time to
pause for reflection and being immune to the diversions of the stage –
the jests and nose-thumbings, the cavortings and indeed the beauty of
the song, 'O mistress mine' with which Feste has just delighted the ears
of revellers and audience alike. Sir Toby is defending a performance-
art, a living entertainment, against a sour-faced outsider: defending the
audience's money's-worth, so to speak. Nevertheless, Shakespeare has
given space for variant interpretation. He himself, after all, was himself
a jumped-up bourgeois: a shareholder in the theatrical company who
was the only actor of his time except Alleyn to make himself a fortune
and buy himself into the ranks of the propertied gentry (he purchased
New Place in 1597), his father having applied for a coat of arms in the
previous year. Greene in *A Groatesworth of Wit* (1592) had stigmatized
him as 'an upstart Crow, beautified with our feathers' ('upstart' because
a mere actor, not a gentleman and a university man). The anonymous
Ratseis Ghost (1605) would comment on the phenomenon of the theatrical parvenu, who lined his pockets till he could 'buy thee some place or
Lordship in the Country . . . Rise up, Sir Simon two shares and a halfe:
Thou art now one of my Knights, and the first Knight that ever was
Player in England . . .' – a player being roughly the social equivalent in
the respectable mind of a vagrant or public nuisance (Honigmann,
E. A. J., *Shakespeare's Impact on his Contemporaries*, pp. 1–13). 'Rise
up, Count Malvolio' ought to be no more and rather less ridiculous. To
participate in the dulcet contagion of the laughter at Malvolio's expense
in *Twelfth Night*, you have to believe that there is something inherently

ludicrous in a steward's aspiration to the hand of a Countess, whereas it is merely understandably foolish that she herself should fall for a servant who is also a disguised girl. You have to collude in Sir Toby's offensive 'Art any more than a steward?' The play does solicit and get this laughter. But the authorial strategy is double and equivocal. For the action exposes, as the practical joke builds towards bursting, the uncivil and uncivilized violence at the root of laughter.

Between the hatching of the 'device' in the rowdy scene 3, and its exercise in scene 5, the poignant musicality of the scene between Orsino and 'Cesario' intervenes and the theatre quietens, holding its breath as Viola unfolds the veiled story of her 'sister's' love. Now again in scene 5, wild, exultant comedy breaks out, all the more powerful for the contrast, in a play so rich in these dappled effects. A new mood of comic orgy prevails, with Malvolio as its comic centre being feasted upon by conspirators and audience alike, while treading the boards of the private theatre of his own imagination, nakedly opened out to the hiders in the box-tree, who implode intermittently at the fantasies their victim acts out. As Malvolio role-plays, comic inversion turns him inside-out, like Feste's 'cheveril glove'. Blatantly but unconsciously, he bares the vulgar depths of his heart's desires, exposing to ridicule the self-flattering content of a luxurious ego-dream, with marvellous specificity – props, supporting cast, costume, speeches, gestures straight from an acting manual. The good steward receives the judgement of comedy – to be baited like a bear (8), tickled like a trout (21–2), caught like a woodcock (83), strung up like a badger (102), flown like a kestrel (112). Maria, that true-bred beagle, is the master of the hunt, controlling the human gaming which, predicated as it is upon a thorough instinct for the processes of the Malvolian psychology, cannot fail to exhibit the predicted mental and behavioural pattern. Here comedy itself is the god: the conspirators invoke the practices of their secret society ('Observe him, for the love of mockery . . . Close, in the name of jesting!' (18; 19–20)), as if they were patron saints or sacred causes. Such a god divines the hidden secrets of the inmost heart with unscrupulous accuracy and in triumphant detail. *Imagination*, which embowers Duke Orsino in a 'high fantastical' aesthetic dream-world and possesses Olivia with a yen for Viola, now converts the poker-faced retainer into 'a rare turkey-cock . . . how he jets under his advanced plumes! . . . he's deeply in. Look how imagination blows him' (30–31; 41–2). Strutting up and down under the compensatory arousal of self-preening fantasies of power and gratification, Malvolio has switched off the censoring mechanism of consciousness and is caught entirely off his guard. His pants are down, metaphorically. We view all. He is human like us, preposterously so.

Fabian's phrase 'he's deeply in' is arresting: suggesting the image of the animal-trap, it also implies the spontaneous withdrawal to the interior life which houses the anarchic springs, desires and energies of life – the theatre of the unconscious whence poetry, madness and infatuation all proceed:

MALVOLIO *Calling my officers about me, in my branched velvet gown, having come from a day-bed, where I have left Olivia sleeping...*

SIR TOBY *Fire and brimstone!*

FABIAN *O, peace, peace!*

MALVOLIO *And then to have the humour of state; and after a demure travel of regard – telling them I know my place, as I would they should do theirs – to ask for my kinsman Toby.*

SIR TOBY *Bolts and shackles!*

FABIAN *O, peace, peace, peace! Now, now!*

MALVOLIO *Seven of my people, with an obedient start, make out for him. I frown the while, and perchance wind up my watch, or play with my – some rich jewel. Toby approaches; curtsies there to me...*

(46–61)

Malvolio's fantasy is a wish-fulfilment compensation for the injuries of humiliation at the hands of Sir Toby rather than a straightforward expression of lust for power or luxury or Olivia. The point of introducing the confected ceremonial, the sycophants and the fine costume (the 'play' Malvolio mentally scripts and stages) is not that Malvolio desires affluence in itself – though, like most people, he would not say no to it – but that his hurt pride takes refuge in a revenge-scenario. *Art any more than a steward?* is answered by a leap into the empyrean of a status equal to 'consanguinity'. Fantasy sets the delighted ego at the centre of the world, serving it up with toadying retainers who hang on one's every word; it licenses patrician negligence, in which arbitrary but benevolent and paternalistic authority may be exercised *sans* obligation, when one will. The gratification of the fantasy increases in proportion to the potency of its realism: gargantuan dreams are grounded in everyday detail. Hence the wicked pleasure we irresistibly take in Malvolio's relish for 'my branched velvet gown' (perhaps he has seen and coveted such a gown, mentally trying it on and admiring its fit and dignity); the 'day-bed' where Olivia sleeps off their conjugal pleasures; the enumeration (not 'several' nor 'some' but '*seven*') of his lackeys who scurry off to do his bidding; the watch and the jewel, tokens of opulent estate – with the sublime slip and hasty correction, as Malvolio remembers that, as Count Malvolio, he won't be wearing his chain of office, which he is evidently in the habit of fingering and has been rudely advised to 'rub with crumbs'. With the obeisance of Sir Toby, who has taken a tumble since the Count's elevation, into the status of a poor relation, 'my kinsman Toby', the fantasy is nearing its peak – a peak from which it must subside into the flatness of everyday reality and the reawakening of grudge and grievance, unless some corroborating circumstance materializes, as indeed the planted letter does. Memorably, the fantasy does not change Malvolio with his assumed role. Bottom with an ass's head is still Bottom the Weaver; he doesn't know what to do with a doting goddess and wants a bottle of hay. Malvolio's pomposity of diction and facial expression ('quenching my familiar smile with an austere regard of control' (65–6)) proclaims him still the steward: a steward masquerading as a count in a steward's dream of greatness. The treatment of the fantasy – punched full of holes by the strangled expostulations of the eavesdroppers – reinforces the conservative structure of the comedy.

The privileged eyes of the spectators, both on-stage and off, look Malvolio through and through. Nobody else in *Twelfth Night* except Sir Andrew (in whom there is nothing to see) is subjected to such caustic X-ray vision. Most just about keep their dignity, even when whirled like a top at the height of folly; only Malvolio is condemned to forfeit his in these central scenes. The fantasies generated by self-love had been noted by Shakespeare himself with chagrin in the grubby recesses of his own inner life:

> Sin of self-love possesseth all mine eye,
> And all my soul, and all my every part;
> And for this sin there is no remedy,
> It is so grounded inward in my heart.
> Methinks no face so gracious is as mine,
> No shape so true, no truth of such account,
> And for myself mine own worth do define,
> As I all other in all worths surmount . . .
>
> (Sonnet 62)

The sonneteer has caught himself performing the equivalent of Malvolio's self-preening in the covert mirror of unworthy self-infatuation. He features it as a form of possession, which takes over the whole ogling organism as it moment-by-moment adores its own reflection, comparing itself to advantage with all comers. But when he consults a genuine mirror, he is floored to see himself in a glass that 'shows me my self indeed, / Beated and chopped with tanned antiquity' (9–10). Weathered and wrinkled, the face that confronts him betrays disfigurement both by age and vanity. His own face is an acute embarrassment. To exorcize this embarrassment he puts it nakedly on exhibition and scourges his vanity by sardonic confession. Malvolio never acquires the wisdom to recognize this constitutional narcissism and thence to redeem it, converting embarrassment to the dignity of good-humoured and forgiving self-knowledge. The comic mirror ruthlessly thrusts back at Malvolio a fool's face, from which he irefully turns away. That very resistance, in Act IV, confers a kind of dignity. In the meanwhile, surely part of the audience's huge laughter as it sees Malvolio exposing his inner life to such ridicule is that of immune recognition: each person's ulterior fantasy-life takes the form of some such low-grade, cheapjack fabrications as Malvolio's, but whereas ours are safely hidden, his are on view. Here but for the Grace of God go . . . you (but *not me* if I can help it).

After perusing the forged letter, Malvolio steps forth from the husk of his old role with sprightly courage. He embraces the future, that heroic bubble, with superb aplomb:

I will be proud, I will read politic authors, I will baffle Sir Toby, I will wash off gross acquaintance, I will be point-devise the very man. I do not now fool myself, to let imagination jade me; for every reason excites to this, that my lady loves me . . .

(155–9)

Five *I will*s in one sentence are thrown off from Malvolio's heady state of excitation, in the form of plans to get up an act capable of knocking Sir Toby clean out of his knighthood (the original meaning of *baffle*). When we next see Malvolio, he will be newly costumed, a yellow shock not only to Olivia's eyeballs but also to all good taste and decorum. 'Point-devise the very man' expresses our crafty itch to play the roles we decide other people want of us, answering what we construe as their 'Wanted' advertisements with the semblance of their imagined hearts'-desires. On next acquaintance, like Bottom, Malvolio will appear 'translated', a comparison which focuses an element of solemn childishness which creeps into the representation Malvolio makes of himself as he acts out his new role – and which indeed is a representation of the way he genuinely thinks of himself. From a tendency to pompous Latinity and recurrent polysyllabic inflation of his native prose, Malvolio passes to a new dialect of child-speech. The psychology of this switch has a forensic precision: day-dream has its roots in infancy, when the world is

103

taken for a mere projection of personal desire. Infantile speech-patterns are already beginning in the *I will* clauses, which mime the ego's vaunted dominance of its environment. In Act III they are magnified in Malvolio's ripostes to his tormentors: the sniffy 'Yes; nightingales answer daws'; the snooty 'Go off, I discard you. Let me enjoy my private. Go off' (4.34–5; 89–90), a regression which is swiftly detected and mocked by the confederacy: 'Why, how now, my bawcock? How dost thou, chuck?' (112–13). Malvolio's utterances, uncensored by reason or sense of humour, have gravitated under the influence of the 'device' to the level of the childhood taunt, 'I'm the king of the castle – get down, you dirty rascal'. Such is the meaning of the pledge in Act II to 'wash off gross acquaintance'.

The Puritan, of course, understood himself to be 'king of the castle', whatever the social class in which he happened to be born. He could enjoy this confidence because he belonged to a minority of the elect, the chosen of God by divine grace and not by his own works, a member of an élite which stood against the vast majority of the reprobate, those dirty rascals disowned by the Creator and predestined for the sulphurous pit. It was calculated that a mere one in a thousand males and one in ten thousand females would make up the community of the elect: the rest, whatever their class or creed, were 'abominations', 'the ungodly', 'fleshpots', 'the children of Sodom'. Maria's 'device' has an infernally funny accuracy in its capacity to locate and stroke that part of the victim's ego which is already inflamed with the notion of Divine Destiny. Malvolio's many references to 'fortune', 'my stars', 'Jove' indicate this bias, which is readily worked upon by the forged letter's invocation of fate and Fortune (143; 152): *'Some are born great, some achieve greatness, and some have greatness thrust upon 'em'* (140–42). If we take Malvolio as 'a kind of puritan' and read 'God' for 'Jove' (see pp. 95–6 above), the Calvinism which underpins Malvolio's self-esteem is clearly exposed:

Jove and my stars be praised! . . . Jove, I thank thee! I will smile. I will do everything that thou wilt have me!

(165–6; 171–2)

And later, in Act III, having assumed the elect stockings, smile and manner, and having been met with utter incredulity, Malvolio (who can no longer interpret anything according to reason but puts a false construction on everything, on the basis of the letter which has become the key to all codes) again lays his high destiny at the door of his Maker:

I have limed her! But it is Jove's doing, and Jove make me thankful! And when she went away now – 'let this fellow be looked to'. Fellow! Not

'Malvolio', nor after my degree, but 'fellow'! Why, everything adheres together, that no dram of a scruple, no scruple of a scruple, no obstacle, no incredulous or unsafe circumstance – what can be said? – nothing that can be, can come between me and the full prospect of my hopes. Well, Jove, not I, is the doer of this, and he is to be thanked.

(III.4.74–83)

The reference to Psalm 118 ('This is the LORD's doing; it is marvellous in our eyes' (23)) invokes a text which the persecuted sects frequently quoted in token of God's special favour and providence:

> The LORD is on my side; I will not fear: what can man do unto me?
> The LORD taketh my part with them that help me: therefore shall I
> see my desire upon them that hate me . . .
> All nations compassed me about; but in the name of the LORD I will
> destroy them . . .
> They compassed me about like bees; they are quenched as the fire of
> thorns: for in the name of the LORD I will destroy them.
> Thou hast thrust sore at me that I might fall: but the LORD helped me.
>
> (Psalm 118:6–7; 10; 12–13)

While avoiding weighting the play with gravity or tainting its levity with religious controversy, Shakespeare's presentation of Malvolio reflects the comic face of George Eliot's Banker Bulstrode and the human face of Jonson's rascally Tribulation Wholesome. This is a self-deceiver who is willing to label his own manipulations ('I have limed her!') with the face-saving sanction of Almighty Providence ('but it is Jove's doing') and the sanctimonious insurance policy of po-faced piety ('and Jove make me thankful!'). The LORD is on his side. But how does one possess such certainty, when one is in a dissident minority of one to at least 999 men and 9,999 women, all encompassing the believer with scorn and hatred? Malvolio, like any Puritan, construes the Divine Will by judicious sifting and weighing of 'signs'. His phraseology, 'dram of a scruple, scruple of a scruple', is conventional Puritan jargon for the Dissenter's scrutiny of the minutiae of everyday experience, to calculate God's will, a procedure which (given the self-deluding mechanisms of even the most strenuous mind) will often yield the desired answer. 'Well, Jove, not I, is the doer of this': Malvolio rests complacent in the favour of Divine Grace, disclaiming the efficacy of his works, handing over both glory and responsibility to the unseen manipulator of his worldly adventures – in short, Maria.

In the Psalm, a member of the persecuted minority feasts on his vindication by a God of revenge. He repeats his intention to 'destroy'

105

his enemies, savouring the idea of firing them out like a swarm of bees. So also Malvolio, in his self-hugging beatitude at his success, looks not only for vindication but for the sweet satisfactions of justified revenge. Within this framework of duplicity and delusion is set forth a panto-mime of a yellow-stockinged, cross-gartered smiler pageanting himself about the stage in one of the most exultantly comic moments in Shake-spearian drama. Olivia looks on incredulously. She has never seen or imagined anything like this. A man who is behaving totally out of character is either out of his mind or acting: Malvolio is madly acting. Yet in a sense he wears the yellow stockings for both of them. Calling for a dose of her saturnine steward as a homoeopathic remedy for her melancholy, Olivia wants the palliative of his company as Orsino needs his music: 'Where's Malvolio? He is sad and civil, / And suits well for a servant with my fortunes' (III.4.5–6). Solemn, bilious and formal, Malvo-lio is constitutionally enrolled under Saturn, the god of melancholy, 'O'erlaid with black, staid Wisdom's hue', as Milton put it in 'Il Penser-oso' (16), and whose companions are 'calm Peace, and Quiet' and 'Spare Fast' (45–6), associated with darkness and solemn cogitation. The Saturnine temperament traditionally opposes the Venerean tempera-ment: it retires coldly from life as that springs forth warmly to love. Both Olivia and Malvolio, having professed the Saturnine way of life, now dedicate themselves to their own opposite: 'ourselves we do not owe' (I.5.300), confesses Olivia, reeling, and goes on to perceive an equivalence between Malvolio's metamorphosis and her own: 'I am as mad as he / If sad and merry madness equal be' (III.4.14–15). The humour of Malvolio's change is made more exquisite when we remem-ber that he would be dressed (as Olivia's retainer, and also as a Puritan) in black, the colour of Saturn and also the colour of mourning, worn by Olivia for her brother, whereas the colour yellow chosen for his transformation (which Olivia, appropriately, has never been able to abide) is iconographically the colour of Venus. Hence Malvolio's preposterous archness as he insinuates his new-made person into her disbelieving eye:

OLIVIA   *Smil'st thou? I sent for thee upon a sad occasion.*

MALVOLIO   *Sad, lady? I could be sad; this does make some obstruction in the blood, this cross-gartering – but what of that? If it please the eye of one, it is with me as the very true sonnet is: 'Please one, and please all'.*

OLIVIA   *Why, how dost thou, man? What is the matter with thee?*

MALVOLIO   *Not black in my mind, though yellow in my legs. It did come*

> *to his hands; and commands shall be executed. I think we do*
> *know the sweet Roman hand.*
>
> OLIVIA   *Wilt thou go to bed, Malvolio?*
> MALVOLIO *To bed! 'Ay, sweetheart, and I'll come to thee!'*
>
> (III.4.18–30)

The play never implies that Malvolio is in love with Olivia, though lust will out, and he persists in talking unconscious bawdry ('Please one, and please all'). His idea of sadness is the mock-heroic gloom engendered by tight garters, but he bears up with fortitude for the sake of the prize. The wincing gallantries of his second speech, with its collusive *we*, its high-flying *his* and its (to Olivia) indeterminate *it*, are the measure of the reckless leap his fantasy has adventured away from commonsense reality. One of the finest comic cross-purpose dialogues in literature finds its consummation in Malvolio's excited belief that, in full light of day, he has been propositioned to get into bed with his employer without further delay. The steward, taking giddy leave of both senses and stewardship, now pounces upon the fruits of his election: 'My Lady' becomes 'sweetheart', to be addressed in the equalizing, familiar *thou*. When Olivia departs, Malvolio addresses his acting virtuosity to the resistance of Sir Toby and his fellow reprobates, who ironically endeavour to exorcize the devil that has possessed him, 'in the name of sanctity' (84). By the end of his participation in this scene, he has been fully and sublimely gulled, stalking around and flapping off the 'idle, shallow things' who exhort him to prayer, for 'I am not of your element. You shall know more hereafter' (122–4). The Chosen of Jove, with his special token of grace, exits prophetically, nose in the air.

Malvolio's 'penance' (136) – the atonement the comedy extorts from him – dominates Act IV, where Malvolio pays to the last farthing the price of his comic hubris and anti-comic solemnity. This is Malvolio's apocalyptic Day of Judgement, locked in a dark room and interrogated by a Clown impersonating a curate, whose black gown without surplice would be recognized as the ironic garb of a Calvinist minister – 'and I would I were the first that ever dissembled in such a gown' (IV.2.5–6). The sanctimonious steward is martyred by the household fool. Foxe's *Book of Martyrs* was always popular reading among Puritans: the elect were aware that they could expect, at best, ridicule in this world, and, at worst, stigmatization, persecution and martyrdom. Such persecution was paradoxically a sign of special grace. Many Puritans knew the inside of a court-house and a gaol but, scorning the judgement of this world, they publicly looked forward to a time when positions would be reversed and the saints would judge their present judges with appropriate ferocity. Malvolio in the darkened room, on trial for his offences against comedy, common sense and the class hierarchy, is the victim of a scene whose disturbed and disturbing resonance has caused sympathy pangs and even admiration for Malvolio and raised reservations and discomfort in the minds of many readers and some viewers as to whether the cruelty of the action runs to excess. Practical jokes, in life as in art, can form channels for sadistic impulses, isolating the victim into temporary panic-stricken helplessness. The Clown's omniscience runs rings round the dark room in which Malvolio is ignorantly and indignantly boxed: his taunting is an exercise of power, designed to bring down the upstart and break his self-command. The imagery set up on the stage – the imprisonment of the inner room surrounded by the free space without – is a graphic representation of the violence sublimated in comedy. Perhaps few scenes have generated such heated controversy. If you take Malvolio's part, you are called a sentimentalist who cannot see or take a harmless joke (that is, you are a bit of a Malvolio yourself). If on the other hand you point out that the scene in the theatre brings the house down, you are accused of being hard-hearted. The turning-point in the interpretation of this scene was Henry Irving's production of *Twelfth Night* in 1884, in which, inspired by Charles Lamb's eloquent essay (see p. 95 above), he modelled the entire production around a 'tragic' exposition of the character of Malvolio, played by himself. A reviewer noted the horror of the 'dark room' in Act IV: 'The mental and physical horror of darkness and the longing yearning for deliverance from a prison cell were never so realized, I think, before'; Malvolio's final lines were spat out in savage rage and left in their wake not the usual ripples of unease but a harsh discordancy which violated the harmonies of the romantic resolution.

Laughter can be near-kin to violence, discharging energy, often involuntarily and subliminally as in the apologetic 'I couldn't help laughing'. This kind of laughter, half-rued after the event, is an explosive gut-reaction. *Twelfth Night*, I have suggested, is a comic reflection and adaptation of conflicts and antipathies deeply and stressfully bound into the society of late Elizabethan England; its laughter converts angry facts into the blessing of laughter. But such laughter is not simply anodyne and benignant. In Act IV, laughter itself, and the psychology of our present laughter in particular, are under scrutiny. As the joke spins out of control, the ache of the solar plexus may turn to a rather uncomfortable labouring with ambivalent emotion. The scene suggests that a line should be drawn between jest and trespass – but where that inscrutable threshold should be is not indicated. Certainly Sir Toby feels that enough has become rather more than enough: 'I would we were well rid of this knavery' (69–70): through his peevish sourness, infantilism is showing, the surface glitter of his wit having rusted off. The scene bristles with emotional contradiction and takes its peculiar power to delight and disturb from that ambiguity. My own experience suggests a profound disjunction between reading-experience and audience-reaction in the proportioning of responses to this ambiguity. As a reader, I have time to pause for thought; in the theatre, time beats us all on like a manic hoop. In reading, I am alone with the page, as Malvolio is alone in the dark, and I, like him, am bent on interpreting this strange experience. Although I, of course, have absolute advantage in knowing why he's there and who is mocking him, I can less readily take advantage of him, for there is no one framed and pinned down in my lens to represent him and I am much employed with the act of interpretation. How am I to 'stage' all this in my mind so as to make sense of it? What are the alternatives? I flick back with my eye, cross-reference, recall, mull over certain pregnant words. Malvolio, as I read his words, is fleetingly myself and I am him: in the quiet interior of my secluded mind, he speaks with my own voice, inflections and dialect – he and I are temporarily assimilated one to the other. What I bring and give, he for that time becomes. In the theatre, a prior act of interpretation has been undertaken: the resonances of private reading are drowned out. Malvolio is not informed by my self but put on and filled out like a glove by some other body and person: detached and autonomous, he travails across yards of board, bombarded by our laughter. There is neither pause for thought nor the wish to impede the momentum of the play's ongoing rhythm, for the play is experienced as process, meaningful in proportion as one is enthralled and diverted.

Most importantly of all, perhaps, I am not alone. The person next to me is suffering mortal convulsions of laughter, and the person next to him is in a similar condition. These shared throes are the essence of the theatrical-experience of *Twelfth Night*. In a sense the Puritans knew more about mass psychology at the public theatre (which held 2,500–3,000 people) than the dramatists liked to admit. Gosson noted that the lower classes:

generally take up a wonderful laughter, and shout altogether in one voice, when they see some notable cozenage practised, or some fly conveyance of bawdry brought out of Italy. Wherby they show themselves rather to like it than to rebuke it.

(in Hazlitt, p. 184)

109

This observation was in answer to the dramatists' claim that their plays were morally edifying. My point is related: judgement can be suspended or censored by comedy, which at once exploits mass psychology and permits no time for the individual's revision of immediate reactions:

MALVOLIO *Sir Topas, never was man thus wronged. Good Sir Topas, do not think I am mad. They have laid me here in hideous darkness –*

FESTE *Fie, thou dishonest Satan! I call thee by the most modest terms, for I am one of those gentle ones that will use the devil himself with courtesy. Sayst thou that house is dark?*

MALVOLIO *As hell, Sir Topas.*

FESTE *Why, it hath bay windows transparent as barricadoes, and the clerestories toward the south-north are as lustrous as ebony. And yet complainest thou of obstruction!*

MALVOLIO *I am not mad, Sir Topas. I say to you, this house is dark.*

(IV.2.28–41)

A reader would have time to sustain the violent shock of Malvolio's predicament, feeling the justice of his outrage (the word *wronged* begins to toll like a bell), admiring his steadiness and certainty under pressure, imagining that 'hideous darkness' from the inside and reflecting on how disorientating it would feel to be held as a lunatic in a dark place and to be told it is light, by an apparent madman in the form of a demonic curate. Political dissidents, the reader might recall, have been punished by internment in asylums for the mad. But the viewing self has no time for such imaginative intimacies: the audience is outside the dark room with Feste, not inside with Malvolio. It is under the influence of the fantastic verbal virtuosities and diverting antics of the Clown, who architects a mad room of the saturnalian imagination in which brilliant impossible light pours through windows of paradox, 'transparent *as barricadoes* . . . clerestories *toward the south-north* . . . lustrous *as ebony*' (emphases added). *Trompe-l'oeil* runs mad as we see in our mind's eye this fantastic fabrication which builds a hall whose magnificently appointed blind windows let in streams of black light from cross-purpose compass points. Feste's wit whirls in manic scintillations, violating the basis of language itself by using similitudes as agents of contrast. Malvolio has been brought, as the penalty for his irrational pride, to the judgement of Non-sense, and there must stand interrogation and trial.

As the interrogation proceeds, so does the sense of Malvolio's real dignity and fortitude under persecution; his ability to hold on, despite the temptation to panic, to the stable bearings of who he is (a sane person of integrity) and where he is (in the dark):

FESTE   *Madman, thou errest. I say there is no darkness but ignorance, in which thou art more puzzled than the Egyptians in their fog.*

MALVOLIO   *I say this house is as dark as ignorance, though ignorance were as dark as hell. And I say there was never man thus abused. I am no more mad than you are – make the trial of it in any constant question.*

FESTE   *What is the opinion of Pythagoras concerning wildfowl?*

MALVOLIO   *That the soul of our grandam might haply inhabit a bird.*

FESTE   *What thinkest thou of his opinion?*

MALVOLIO   *I think nobly of the soul, and no way approve his opinion.*

FESTE   *Fare thee well; remain thou still in darkness. Thou shalt hold the opinion of Pythagoras ere I will allow of thy wits, and fear to kill a woodcock lest thou dispossess the soul of thy grandam. Fare thee well.*

(IV.2.42–59)

Malvolio speaks for Christian stability against pagan transformation. His affirmation 'I think nobly of the soul, and no way approve his opinion' is an arresting moment in which Malvolio's gravity and self-esteem, which have suffered such a comic battering in the course of the play, take on (both in the reading and in many performances) a noble quality. As against the humiliating metamorphosis he has suffered, Malvolio possesses his own soul again: his dignified answer resolutely affirms the foundation of Christian value and extracts it from the human vanities with which it is overlaid. But just as I am pondering this statement of belief, the person in the seat next to me begins to splutter at Feste's swiftly ensuing joke about the woodcock and the soul of Malvolio's grandmother. The image of Malvolio as a vegetarian-to-be dissolves the mood in comedy. Thus the viewing self is never allowed to rest in the solidity of the moment but must be hurried on in the fluent, changeful process of the play's chiaroscuro dynamics, each event begetting the next in a volatile play of swift repartee and oscillating moods. This restless, galvanizing, de-forming and re-creating spirit is embodied in Feste: it figures here in the theme of Pythagorean metempsychosis, the Renaissance type for the instability of all life – from Marlowe's *Dr Faustus*, 'Ah, Pythagoras' metempsychosis, were that true . . .' (V.ii.184) to Jonson's burlesque of 'the soul of Pythagoras,

/ That juggler divine' in Act I of *Volpone*, whose transmigrations include the form of 'a precise, pure, illuminate brother' (a Puritan), otherwise known as an ass (I.ii.6–7, 43). In the Feste–Malvolio dialogue, the steward who speaks nobly of the soul may arrest the reader in mid-flight and achieve the triumph of the saints, but Feste's smart answers will take the viewer by storm and get in the final word.

In the concluding Act, Malvolio's demand for retribution ruffles the tranquillizing tunefulness of the romantic ending with a final, ireful demand for explanation and redress. He is met at first with Olivia's solicitude and a desire to rectify what he has so scandalously suffered. But the politic Fabian is allowed to intervene, owning up but offering the palliative conclusion that there were faults on both sides and that this 'sportful malice . . . May rather pluck on laughter than revenge' (363–4). Olivia's attitude modulates to one of amused compassion, most galling to the already smarting ego of the comic victim: 'Alas, poor fool! How have they baffled thee!' (367), unconsciously equating Malvolio with his leering mirror-image in the Fool himself, who now chimes in vigorously and vengefully, ending in his famous aphorism: 'thus the whirligig of time brings in his revenges' (373–4). The comic top of Time corresponds with the tragic wheel of Fortune. Its violent revolutions delight only those who willingly play the game and concur in the enjoyment of 'sportful malice' – that is, the conspirators and most of the audience, most of the time. For those who pity the baited bear, there is no option but to flounce out of the fun with Malvolio in his immortal *Exit*.

6. Boy–girls and Girl–boys: Sexual Indeterminacy

Sexual ambivalence has immemorially been associated with the theatre. Suetonius, the Roman historian, remarked on 'the licentious behaviour of stage-players': the Emperor Augustus, hearing that Stephanio, an actor, 'went about attended by a page-boy who was really a married woman, with her hair cropped ... had him flogged through all the three theatres – those of Pompey, Balbus, and Marcellus – and then exiled' (*The Twelve Caesars*, II). In Shakespeare's day, Puritans became heated about 'filthiness':

The Law of God very straitly forbids men to put on women's apparell, garments are set down for signs distinctive between sex and sex ... All that do so are abhomination to the Lord; which way, I beseech you, shall they be excused that put on, not the apparell only, but the gate, the gestures, the voice, the passions of a woman?

(Gosson, Stephen, *The Confutation of Plays*, in Hazlitt, p. 195)

Philip Stubbes in *The Anatomie of Abuses* called the players 'double dealing ambodexters', violating the laws of nature and of God by their use of boy-actors to impersonate women. These boy–girls were tainted with the allure of the forbidden fruit of pederasty. They challenged by their defiance of gender norms the inscription by patriarchal culture of sexual difference as an invariable law, immutable and fixed, implying that the human male was not born with breeches but later inserted into them and acculturated to his role, costume and behaviour. The signs of masculinity were fetched from an arbitrary wardrobe and could be discarded at will. Such flighty deviance from the assumed codes on which the social hierarchy and individual identity depended would not just seem distasteful but 'abhomination to the Lord', challenging Genesis itself: 'Male and female created he them.'

The pederastic implications of theatrical cross-dressing were not, as I shall show, merely the product of the febrile imaginings of Puritans: they were real enough, but subtle and, in the case of Shakespearian comedy, part of a complex tissue of aestheticism whose warp contradicted its weft. No other Renaissance English dramatist showed the same fascination as Shakespeare for the double cross-dressing motif: its charm and potency seemed inexhaustible, for he returned to the boy–girl–boy figure in *The Two Gentlemen of Verona* (Julia), *As You Like It*

(Rosalind), *The Merchant of Venice* (Portia and Jessica) and the late *Cymbeline* (Imogen). In *Twelfth Night*, the Viola/'Cesario' figure reflects in his/her/his face the dreamlike mirrorings of a play which meditates the likeness people desire – and, because they desire, intuit – between themselves and others; it concentrates the comedy's self-reflexive concern with acting, role-play, human nature as a fluid art-work in the eyes of the beholder. Viola is a shape-changer, an embodied metamorphosis, an elegant variation on the Renaissance humanist delight in fluid indeterminacy as the most essentially human characteristic. In Pico's vastly influential *Oration: On the Dignity of Man*, God 'the best of artists' remedies his omission in forgetting to include Adam in the initial creation by inventing man 'as a creation with an unspecified image': man accordingly is undetermined, shapeless (or shape-free) and without a fixed role; he may, by trial and error, try on all possible roles and discard them at will, 'the moulder and maker of yourself'. 'Who would not admire this chameleon of ours?' cries out Pico, admiring man as 'a multiform being of an inconstant nature', as a consummate actor on the stage of this world (in Davies, S., *Renaissance Views of Man*, pp. 67–9). But disguise, as Viola, wide-eyed acknowledges, is a 'wickedness' (II.2.27). This readily acknowledged truism, informing Renaissance literature from *The Faerie Queene* to *Volpone*, was summed up in the person of Proteus, the water-god, the type of transformation, whose form is to be formless, the slippery image of a world of untrustworthy surfaces. In the earliest of Shakespeare's 'androgyne' plays, the fickle hero's name is Proteus, whose faithlessness to Julia all but engenders her transformation to 'Sebastian' in the effort to win him back. *Two Gentlemen* is as close in its way to *Twelfth Night* as is *The Comedy of Errors*, with Orsino acting as the latter play's Proteus – less coarsely mercurial and exploitative but wavering and formless as the sea which borders Illyria and is a recurrent focus of his own imagery and that used by the Clown to describe him (see p. 64 above). In both comedies there is sharp irony in the inconsistency of the protean male (carrying the stigma patriarchy attaches to women, *varium et mutabile semper*, and garrulous too), and the stable and rational behaviour of the girl–boy 'ambodexter' within her deceptive costume. But his cryptic use of the boy-actor playing the girl–boy heroine goes further than mere reversal: it extends female characterization into a realm which confounds sex-differentiation. Viola impersonates Pico's definition of man himself, 'a creation with an unspecified image', 'the moulder and maker of yourself', 'this chameleon of ours', 'a various multiform being'. Viola is the play's quandary; she equals X, throwing all in doubt by maintaining a destabilizing and ambiguous existence in a fixed social order which is intolerant of and inimical to *arrivistes*, on whom it pounces, to strip them of decent camouflage down to pitiful nudity. Frankly, Viola gets away with being a liar and a fixer, a manipulative dissembler who not only steals the prize of a Ducal husband but also ingratiates herself into the good graces of the audience, which considers her to be impeccably honourable and thoroughly endearing. The playwright, Viola and the audience share a special dispensation of cakes and ale, unlike Malvolio, Sir Andrew and Antonio: we have them and eat them too. How and why is this conjuration managed?

Ambiguity and illusionism are the very substance of the theatrical-experience, especially in a play like *Twelfth Night*, where *trompe-l'oeil* in the form of identical twins is centre-stage. The character of Viola is made sexually attractive to the audience while at the same time sustaining an extraordinary aura of innocence. This is so whether the actor is a boy or a woman, though responses are likely to differ significantly in either case. Both our sexual response and our sense of the character's immunity to adverse criticism derive from her/his sexual indeterminacy: the girl–boy kindles fantasy but solicits affection by the intimation of pre-sexual androgynous youthfulness s/he carries with her/him. Most of us will never have the chance to see the play in the way it was designed, that is, with the boy-actor biasing the homoerotic undertones towards the pederastic. There would be at once fewer veils of sexual suggestiveness in the original – since a boy representing a girl playing a boy is imitating a version of himself – and a greater number, since the layers of illusion deepen the sense of indeterminacy. In a modern version in which Viola is played by a young woman, some but not all of the pederastic implication is forfeited: the Antonio/Sebastian plot maintains the theme. But the homoerotic resonances are just as powerful, weighting the play's suggestions of lesbian attraction in the feminine mirrorings of the Viola/Olivia relationship, which can be deeply and subtly exciting on a sexual level. Indeed, Sapphic love, though not a major preoccupation of the period as was male homosexual love and same-sex friendship, was understood as an aspect of Eros. Donne's Sappho, caressing herself in the mirror, imagines her girlfriend's body:

> My two lips, eyes, thighs, differ from thy two,
>   But so, as thine from one another do;
> And, oh, no more; the likeness being such,
>   Why should they not alike in all parts touch?
> Hand to strange hand, lip to lip none denies;
>   Why should they breast to breast, or thighs to thighs?

> Likeness begets such strange self flattery,
> That touching myself, all seems done to thee . . .
> O cure this loving madness, and restore
> Me to me; thee, my half, my all, my more.
> ('Sappho to Philaenis', 45–52; 57–8)

Though very evidently written to titillate and gratify a male voyeur, Donne's dramatic monologue recognizes the fascination between female affinities and mirrorings which modern representations of *Twelfth Night* also make available to their audiences. 'Thy tongue, thy face, thy limbs, actions, and spirit / Do give thee fivefold blazon', muses Olivia when Viola has quit her house (I.5.281–2), demonstrating the degree to which she has looked the youth up and down, admiring not only the tokens of gentility in language and manner but also the shape of 'his' legs. Whereas Renaissance audiences saw through to a 'real' boy in either case, the legs we see are womanly, and pleasing to the female beholder. Such delectable sexual suggestions (tactfully underwritten as they are) are also deepened and complicated for modern viewers by the feminist implications which are released by the cross-dressing motif when the actor is a woman. We view the extent to which that which society has constructed as proper to the male is also present in the female: the 'boy' in the 'girl' is liberated to play the most active role in the whole play.

The impression we have of special intimacy with Viola is born of the dramatic irony which bonds us with this character in exactly the ratio that she is estranged and hidden from the other persons. Her soliloquistic loneliness, reverie, good feeling, wit, gentle gallantry and general helplessness have a special poignancy for the audience because we take them personally: they have been confided to us. But this greater knowledge does not imply that the riddle of Viola's sexual identity is eliminated for us. On the contrary, the tantalizing and enigmatically attractive 'something' divined by Orsino and Olivia in 'Cesario', to which we have the theoretical key, is provocatively and seductively present to us whenever she is on-stage. Like Rosalind in *As You Like It* (but not Portia in *The Merchant of Venice* whose 'maleness' consists in the concealing cloak of professionalism as law-giver), Viola invites our eyes to dwell upon her body, since her gender is consistently the ulterior topic of conversation when she is present. The character is presented as sexually attractive enough to appeal to the latent homosexual or bisexual in each member of the audience. It offers a licit and playful version of a transgressive desire or 'fancy' (to use the parlance of the play), permitting sanctuary to sexual inclinations which, however, are given an almost childlike rightness within the safety of the dramatic decorum. *Twelfth Night* bears witness to having been written by the author of the bisexual Sonnets where a 'lovely boy' is the cynosure of all eyes. But in Viola/'Cesario' it offers an image of sexual totality in which each viewer may find a reflection at once lovable and desirable: s/he can be all things to all men and all women, but with the double safeguard that what you are seeing is only a reflection and an illusion; that the tone is chaste and modest; that sexual norms will reassert themselves in due course. If Viola equals X, then X equals both likeness and opposition, homo- and hetero-sexuality, *What you will*. Quiller-Couch congratulated Shakespeare on having created a comedy refreshingly free of bawdry (in Cambridge University Press edn, p. xix) – an irony in view of the fact that this play is suffused with sexuality throughout. And yet the comment does respond to something very real in the texture of the play – a quality of profound innocence which the playwright scrupulously imparts to the transactions and persons of Illyria. The homoerotic content is rendered permissible and licit to the audience because of its confinement to the realm of the imagination, sensitively suggested without gross suggestiveness, and because it implies a pre-sexual and delicately reticent experience of identification, set in the matrix of familial bondings of close and tender brother–sister, sister–sister and big brother–little brother relationships, whether real or metaphorical. The play cherishes its lovers for their youthfulness, and especially Viola, as adolescents on their way to mature (that is, conservative and orthodox) bondings.

More often than by any other attribute, Viola is addressed or mentioned by the other characters in terms of her youth – a 'Dear lad' (I.4.29) to Orsino; the 'mother's milk . . . scarce out of him' in Malvolio's opinion' (5.156); 'this youth's perfections' to Olivia (5.285); 'boy' (II.4.15; 25); 'my boy' (118); 'the lamb that I do love' (V.1.128), evoking the precious 'one ewe-lamb' of II Samuel which the poor man in the parable 'had bought and nourished up: and it grew up together with him, and with his children; it did eat of his own meat, and drank of his own cup, and lay in his bosom, and was unto him as a daughter' (12:3). In the midst of the whimsy and pure play that has the audience laughing, and not dissociated from the winning and beguiling sexuality of Viola, lies the deep-rooted and protective affection she calls up. On the quicksilver borderline of adolescence, Viola/'Cesario' can stand for the evanescent moment in a person's life when s/he is most vulnerable, open and in process of change (in the case of a male) from the mother's son to the father's image – a suspended moment in which female and male identities can seem to merge and melt. The haunting simplicity of her speech reinforces this sense of youthful

117

openness. It is not that she speaks childishly but rather that her speech-patterns, though superficially riddling and cryptic, have a syntactic plainness that disarms the audience by its trustful confidingness. Whereas the playwright's dramatic strategy manipulated us into discharging our laughter at poor Malvolio, it manoeuvres us into protective partiality for this gamin waif whose grave simplicity is coupled with feelings of restrained helplessness, appealing to the audience's protective instincts and cajoling us into according preferential treatment:

> *I left no ring with her; what means this lady?*
> *Fortune forbid my outside have not charm d her!*
> *She made good view of me, indeed so much*
> *That – me thought – her eyes had lost her tongue . . .*
> *She loves me, sure . . .*
> *Poor lady, she were better love a dream.*
> *Disguise, I see thou art a wickedness*
> *Wherein the pregnant enemy does much.*
> *How easy is it for the proper false*
> *In women's waxen hearts to set their forms.*
> *Alas, our frailty is the cause, not we,*
> *For such as we are made, if such we be . . .*
>
> (II.2.17–20; 22; 27–32)

The impression artfully fostered by this soliloquy is of artless naïveté as the protagonist argues her laborious way to the glaringly obvious conclusion, 'She loves me, sure . . .', emitting expressions of rueful compassion for her victim: 'Fortune forbid . . .', 'Poor lady . . .' The air of ingenuousness covers and extenuates the imposture she practises. Likewise when she exclaims so unaffectedly over her discovery of the essential wickedness of disguise (a moral fact known, after all, to most five-year-olds) the poetry effectively washes her hands of the taint of such devilry in the very process of admitting it. We are led to accept her as an innocent caught up in her role, as if this had indeed been conferred by the external agency of 'Fortune' and must inevitably be confided to the equally external ministrations of 'time' (40). The poet's master-minding dodges are reinforced by the bare-faced childishness of the boy-actor, who could play the innocent with natural gaucherie. The ambidextrousness of the rhetoric is given further complexity by the near swerve towards the end of the quoted speech by which Viola moves from pity for Olivia as her unintended victim to identification with her as fellow-woman (and hence fellow-victim). She elides her predicament with Olivia's in a formal couplet (31–2) in which *our* and *we* recur no less than four times. By this sleight the gap between her actions and her responsibility for their consequences is closed, while the gap between 'self' and 'role', boy-actor playing girl, girl playing boy, is ironically opened. The problematics of sex in the double-gendered 'Cesario' ('As I am man . . .' 'As I am woman . . .' (36; 38)), and the audience's uninhibited enjoyment of this ambivalence, come to the forefront of the speech. In excluding any whisper of sexual obscenity, the play opens safe gates to a dream-world of mesmerizingly shot-silk sexuality, giving permission to wandering but endeared eyes and roving but guilt-free fancies. *Twelfth Night* further ensures the tranquillity of such pleasures by its emphasis on transient festive play, assimilating the class- and gender-reversals of the traditional Roman Saturnalia, the Feast of Fools, the Boy-Bishop and carnival. The Saturnalia re-enacted the lost golden age of Saturn by reversing hierarchy; in England, transvestism was common at Shrove:

> Both men and woman chaunge their weede, the men in maydes aray,
> And wanton wenches drest like men, doe travel by the way.

The 'goldenness' of *Twelfth Night* is a festive mood which bathes the central girl–boy in festive and all-forgiving light.

Modern readers and viewers have responded to the feminist implications of Shakespeare's cross-dressing women, for whom the adoption of male clothing, linguistic freedom and behaviour is felt as an experiment in liberation from the custodial sentence bestowed by society on women. In *Twelfth Night* such an analysis does not really work but its very inadequacy sheds an interesting light on the play. It is true that Shakespeare was writing in a period of surging social change affecting also the status and claims of women, a challenge which his plays reflect. Social fashions challenged the fixed distinctions of gender: effeminate men and mannish women were much complained of, as in William Harrison's *Description of England* (1587) which draws scandalized and fascinated attention to females wearing 'doublets with pendant codpieces on the breast . . . galligaskins to bear out their bums . . . it hath passed my skill to discern whether they were men or women'. For the Puritan Stubbes, such women were 'hermaphrodites and monsters', a word which Viola echoes in her soliloquy (34) (in Edward Berry, *Shakespeare's Comic Rites*, p. 96). However, Viola's character bears no relation to the rebellious females strutting around London (or was it just through Harrison's electric imagination?) in their bullish doublets and dangling codpieces. Like that of the boy-page Julia in *Two Gentlemen of Verona*, Viola's romance get-up is no enfranchisement into the greater world of male action. Ironically, her disguise leads to little but confusion and choicelessness; Olivia, sole lord of her household, has far more authority than Viola, even to the point of aggressively haling Viola's twin off to betrothal. The beauty of Viola lies in plainsong monody, trapped in the irony of a male garb behind which she must imitate the passivity ordained by society for women and children. While Portia dominates Act IV of *The Merchant of Venice* as an embodied *Iustitia*, balancing the scales and sword of Justice after the model of Queen Elizabeth as Astraea, goddess of Justice, and while Rosalind in *As You Like It* conducts with panache the education of Orlando in her pose as Ganymede, Viola is an errand-boy, the tool of Orsino, and the 'fool' of Olivia (III.1.141). Far from implying feminist rebellion against Elizabethan sex-roles, Viola's behaviour, manner of speech, social position and supposed age combine to duplicate the traditional inferiority of female status. As a 'boy' and household dependant, she may be taken into the Duke's confidence and can assert her status as a 'gentleman' (I.5.268), but she remains a youthful subordinate and employee. In the Duke's presence, she is subdued and reserved under his patronage, the recipient of orders and the receptacle of confidences. Orsino's first conversation with her in Act I, scene 4, is conducted almost exclusively in the imperative mood:

> *Therefore, good youth,* address *thy gait unto her.*
> Be *not denied access;* stand *at her doors,*
> *And* tell *them, there thy fixed foot shall grow*
> *Till thou have audience.*
>
> (15–18; emphases added)

Like an imperious actor's prompt-book, he directs and scripts her actions: '*Be* clamorous', '*leap* all civil bounds', '*unfold* the passion', '*Surprise* her', '*attend* it' (21; 24; 25; 27; emphases added). Throughout, she says little to the Duke's much, maintaining a quiet presence which has such resonance on-stage precisely because of its enforced suppressions and withholdings. Such time-biding endurance is the classic stance of the feminine, a variation on the patient Griselda icon. Her disguise ironically replicates the constraints society imposes on women: a deferential stilling of the clacking tongue (otherwise you are a 'scold' or a 'gossip') and the maintenance of a receptive passivity. In the scenes with Olivia and the Clown, Viola's freedom to speak and to play a vividly active part is in tension with an impression of painful reserve; wretched unease is generated by the incompatibility between the explicit and the implicit in what she says and does. Thus her eloquent tribute to her rival's beauty (I.5.228 ff.) brims with unspoken rue; her simple 'I pity you' tells much of inner pain (III.1.120). The impression of a hidden life is always with us – a hiddenness which is the stereotypical role of woman. Again, the duelling trick reveals in Viola the trembling discomfiture appropriate to the conventionally female temperament: unnerved, she is also unmanned, to the degree that 'A little thing would make me tell them how much I lack of a man' (III.4.294–5). The innuendo draws attention to the fact that she is not sexually accoutred for any kind of martial or amorous enterprise, 'a little thing' implying the male member, the 'foolish thing' of Feste's song, that 'something to my purpose nothing' of the Sonnets, whereby the Young Man is 'pricked out' for women's pleasure (20). 'Cesario', who is not 'pricked out', parodies the fashionable cult of the Spenserian 'martial maid', based on the cults of Diana, Minerva and Venus Armata, iconographically representing Elizabeth as warrior queen. Whereas Spenser's Britomart in *The Faerie Queen* will knock you down as soon as look at you, in a poem which does not equate potency with possession of a phallus, gentle Viola shakes and squirms. Britomart leaves a trail of blood baths in her wake. Here she is encountering the rather harmless Marinell on the sea shore:

> But she againe him in the shield did smite
> With so fierce furie and great puissance,
> That through his threesquare scuchin percing quite,
> And through his mayled hauberque by mischaunce
> The wicked steele through his left side did glaunce;
> Him so transfixed she before her bore
> Beyond his croupe, the length of all her launce,
> Till sadly soucing on the sandie shore,
> He tombled on an heape, and wallowd in his gore.
>
> (III.iv.16)

Whereas Britomart's 'wicked steele' has power to penetrate her victim up to the hilt, 'Cesario' when urged to 'strip [her] sword stark naked' (III.4.244–5) shows an entire lack of wherewithal:

> *This is as uncivil as strange . . .*
> *I am one that had rather go with Sir Priest than Sir Knight; I care not*
> *who knows so much of my mettle.*
>
> (247; 264–6)

This poor little brag ('I care not') represents a last-ditch attempt to cover her embarrassment with a few rags of macho diction. The point of the comedy is that, though 'Cesario' goes armed as a sign of being a gentleman, the Viola 'he' contains and costumes has no 'sword' in her underwear to be 'stripped stark naked', since prowess is constructed as essentially male according to the cant pun on 'penis' and 'weapon'. The reactionary tendency of the gender-comedy of *Twelfth Night* is in constant dialogue with its feint at liberation from norms. Laughter in this scene depends on our indulgent assumption that women are naturally effeminate, and that they are so not just because they have not been trained in martial arts but because they lack the basic anatomical artillery. This comedy would be only slightly complicated by the use of a boy-actor, for although the youth would be suitably equipped, such untried equipment might be thought to be virginally immature – another equation of women and children, as allowable cowards. This reinforcement of gender-stereotypes is pleasantly complicated by the awful fright of Sir Andrew at being matched with the 'firago' youth, for puny Sir Andrew seems equally lacking in the area of prowess. If Viola is not much of a man, neither is he, when you come down to it. Within the gender-conventions which underpin the comedy, he is constructed as yet another female impersonator.

Twelfth Night therefore presents its sexually indeterminate pairings – 'Cesario' and Orsino, Viola and Olivia, Sebastian and Antonio – not to provide feminist illuminations but to play upon homoerotic feelings which it would not have been possible to present explicitly on the Elizabeth stage, or on any stage since then, until the legalization of male homosexuality. Sodomy, which became a criminal act under Henry VIII, punishable by burning, had found provocative voice only in Marlowe's *Edward II*, with its dramatization of forbidden fantasies played out tragically in the theatre of political life:

> Sometime a lovely boy in Dian's shape,
> With hair that gilds the water as it glides,
> Crownets of pearl about his naked arms,
> And in his sportful hands an olive-tree,
> To hide those parts which men delight to see,
> Shall bathe him in a spring; and there, hard by,
> One like Actaeon, peeping through the grove,
> Shall by the angry goddess be transform'd,
> And running in the likeness of an hart,
> By yelping hounds pull'd down, and seem to die . . .
>
> (I.i.61–70)

Gaveston, mulling over the stage-direction of the 'pliant king's' life so as to convert it into a libidinous art-form like that of Tiberius on Capri, in which catamites are boy-actors impersonating the lusciously forbidden goddess Diana, imagines the manipulation of his royal patron by the method of turning life into masque. The trope of peeping Actaeon, which also opens *Twelfth Night* as an emblem of frustrated yearning, connotes the dangerous pleasure of the illicit ('*hard* by' can be read as a sexual pun on Actaeon's throbbing desire, and 'seem to *die*' another orgiastic innuendo), but ironically foreshadows the brutal fate of both king and minion. By contrast, Orsino's use of the Actaeon motif ('That instant was I turned into a hart, / And my desires, like fell and cruel hounds, / E'er since pursue me' (I.1.22–4)) has a self-reflexive inwardness which insists on the autonomy of the imagination: transgressive desires will never be enacted. If the Actaeon story constitutes a sign of the forbidden, *Twelfth Night* uses it to signal the safe limits of its licence.

Within these limits, the play gives voice to feelings engendered by the cult of male friendship and love which enjoyed a heyday in Elizabethan England, especially within the homosexual subculture on whose margins Shakespeare moved – the society of Southampton, Oxford, Bacon, Lord Henry Howard – a cult only less culturally fashionable than that of Athens in the fourth century B.C. This society was almost exclusively male, openly expressive of amorous affection, and given to philosophical and introspective speculation. Its values and manners were founded on those of the male love celebrated in Plato's *Symposium* and *Phaedrus*, understood as the attachment of an older to a younger man, the boy bringing beauty to the partnership and the older acting as mentor:

The man who would pursue the right way to this goal must begin, when he is young, by applying himself to the contemplation of physical beauty, and, if he is properly directed by his guide, he will first fall in love with one particular beautiful person and beget noble sentiments in partnership with him.

(*The Symposium*, 210)

As Plato elaborates, it becomes clear that the boy is endowed with qualities socially constructed as 'feminine' (though women are despised as a lower order, capable of bearing merely fleshly children) and the older man with 'masculine' attributes. The value put on the ambiguity of youth both in classical times and in Elizabethan England is reflected in the figure of Narcissus, whose story is both restated and restructured in *Twelfth Night* (see pp. 53,59 above). The melancholy narrative of Narcissus as told by Ovid presents a classic instance of the bisexual attractiveness of the young male:

For when yeares three times five and one he fully lived had,
So that he seemde to stande betweene the state of man and Lad,

> The hearts of divers trim young men his beautie gan to move,
> And many a Ladie fresh and faire was taken in his love.
> (Ovid, *Metamorphoses*, (III.438–41), trans. Golding, A. (1565–7))

Both Viola and her twin brother reflect this much-ogled and coveted Narcissus. On one side of Viola stands that trim young man Orsino; on the other the 'Ladie fresh and faire' Olivia, with 'Cesario' seducing the eyes of both male and female. This threefold grouping is paralleled by the attraction exerted on Antonio on the one hand and later Olivia on the other. The symmetry, however, is imperfect: Sebastian, like Orsino, by *trompe-l'oeil* illusionism, is made to appear to get craftily older as the play proceeds. Though the whole play is grounded on his literal identity with Viola (same height, same face, same treble voice) his gruff, macho and pugilistic behaviour contradicts this identity, and he refers to Viola as if they had different ages (V.1.245). The idea of twinhood is in practice a floating fiction, as blurred as the sexual indeterminacy it signals. This is presumably because the playwright is preparing the plot for the conventions of heterosexual matrimony, in which (as Orsino explains to 'Cesario') the wife is expected to be younger than the husband. Calling such categorical imperatives into question, the play nevertheless gestures submission to them in the twins' double marriage.

Twelfth Night is preoccupied with the means of representation. It centres attention in Act I, scene 5, on Olivia's veiled face. She lifts the veil; the unveiling reveals the possibility of an underlying illusion, for it discloses the boy-actor. In the original performance, the lad playing Viola had an easier job than the one playing Olivia, for he could more nearly impersonate himself, both sexually and in age, the cross-dresser cross-dressing to mime the image of a feminized male like Narcissus, whereas to represent Olivia, the pubescent boy must feign his own opposite. When Olivia undertakes to 'draw the curtain and show you the picture' (of 'her' face) (223), that face is a picture indeed, for it is no woman's face but a simulation. Viola's 'Excellently done – if God did all' (226) draws sour attention to the possibilities of cosmetic intervention, which Olivia breezily disowns. The scene, with its multiple nuanced play on feigning and double-feigning, play-acting, portraiture, fabrication, riddles, printing and counterfeiting, and layer upon layer of sexual ambivalence, relates closely to the situation of Shakespeare's Sonnets in which the poet-persona woos the Narcissan young man first to breed copies of himself and then to unite in love with poet:

> VIOLA *'Tis beauty truly blent, whose red and white*
>   *Nature's own sweet and cunning hand laid on.*

> *Lady, you are the cruellest she alive,*
> *If you will lead these graces to the grave,*
> *And leave the world no copy.*
>
> (I.5.228–32)

Nature's paintbrush worked the natural artifice of Olivia's skin-tones, copying (Platonistically) from the true pattern in the Form or Idea of Beauty. The boy-actor simulates this art-work. Erasmus's *Praise of Marriage* had reminded the beautiful of their duty to procreate, thus generating *copies* of themselves, a trope with which Shakespeare opens his sonnet-sequence, urging the Young Man to disseminate his own image with all due celerity: 'Die single, and thine image dies with thee' (3); 'Make thee another self for love of me' (10), for Nature 'carved thee for her seal, and meant thereby / Thou shouldst print more, not let that copy die' (11). Insemination as a printing process to print more issue, or as a form of capital investment to increase the currency, is presented in the first fourteen sonnets as the antidote to the sterility of remaining 'contracted to thine own bright eyes' (1) – the initial situation of the two major protagonists in *Twelfth Night*. The beloved of the Sonnets is not unlike Orsino, a self-hoarding Narcissus who has to be cajoled out of his self-sealed immunity as a musical melancholic ('Music to hear, why hear'st thou music sadly?' (8)). From urging the merely carnal and extempore mimesis of begetting, Shakespeare moves to the offer of his own art as an eternal imprint of an indelible beauty (15) together with a passionate statement of emotional bonding, sexual attraction and needy, insecure desire for a lover who is sexually ambivalent:

> A woman's face, with Nature's own hand painted,
> Hast thou, the master-mistress of my passion;
> A woman's gentle heart, but not acquainted
> With shifting change, as is false woman's fashion . . .
>
> (20)

The beauty of the beloved is represented as inimitable, even by the accepted archetypes of beauty, whether male or female:

> Describe Adonis, and the counterfeit
> Is poorly imitated after you;
> On Helen's cheek all art of beauty set,
> And you in Grecian tires are painted new.
>
> (53)

Hyperbolical compliments fly, admiring a bisexual beauty that transcends gender-norms; soft-faced Adonis and voluptuous Helen both supply shadows of the beloved's allure. But the flattery is shot through with doubt and needling, half-suppressed cynicisms. It is a language which 'counterfeits' 'imitations'. The homoerotic lover of the Sonnets is the frantic, casuistical questor in pursuit of a fleeing self-projection which always finally denies or eludes him. A raw and angry pain burns at the heart of the sequence at the sham and let-down located both in the young man and in the self that desires to unite with him.

In *Twelfth Night* this failure of homoerotic fulfilment is located not in the major plot but in the minor Antonio/Sebastian action. This constitutes the most troubled area of the comedy, not only in its oblique exposition of the sonnet themes but in the variable quality of the writing, which seems to strain in its search for adjustment to the graceful lightness of the major cadencing. The plot reinforces the theme of search for an *alter ego* in a drama where shadows of shadows, images of disguised images, restlessly seek authentic likenesses or doubles. Homoerotic linkings imply scintillating possibilities of a self located beyond the self, but these the play construes as uncanny echoes only, always diaphanously unreal and evasively out of reach. Antonio's hot pursuit of Sebastian sounds the bass note of this theme of obsessive search in the most passionate and passionately discordant relationship of the play. The exposition of their relationship opens with their imminent parting: the beloved is abandoning the lover. The *Twelfth Night* trope of loss, search and flight is married in this underplot to the larger Shakespearian concerns of ingratitude, betrayal and guilt; the emergence of the boy-twin into the main plot spreads a ripple-effect of these emotions into the other relationships, to climax in Antonio's rage with Viola mistaken for Sebastian in Act V, and the detonation of a corresponding explosion in Orsino for Viola as 'Cesario'. Since the ingratitude, betrayal and guilt turn out to be figments based on mistaken identity (known, of course, to the audience), these emotions can be allowed into play within the calculated immunity of the comic framework. Antonio emerges as a vulnerable, lacerated man, from first to last a loser and alien. The rawest, most devoted and possessive love in the play belongs to him, so that an emotional centre of *Twelfth Night* is located on its margins. 'Male friendship' is too weak a term for this absolute bonding between young men which fascinated Shakespeare all his writing life, from *Two Gentlemen* where Valentine offers his lady to his cheating rival in token of reconciliation, to *The Winter's Tale* in which the lifelong friendship between Leontes and Polixenes, the 'twinned lambs' of infancy (I.2.62) contains an element of pathological self-identification on Leontes' part.

Antonio's first speech is an attempt to detain Sebastian from leaving him: 'Will you stay no longer? Nor will you not that I go with you?' (II.1.1–2). From his first line, he is condemned to the role of frustrated lover of a young man whose obstinate determination to rove off alone is ballasted by no good reason, and is presented in a rhetoric of stylized, formal and mannered courtesy so studied that it might have come straight from a book of gentlemanly etiquette. Sebastian is Castiglione's courtier beating a polite but determined retreat:

SEBASTIAN   *By your patience, no. My stars shine darkly over me. The*
             malignancy of my fate might perhaps distemper yours;
             therefore I shall crave of you your leave, that I may bear
             my evils alone. It were a bad recompense for your love to
             lay any of them on you.
ANTONIO   *Let me yet know of you whither you are bound.*
SEBASTIAN   *No, sooth, sir; my determinate voyage is mere*
             extravagancy.

                                                              (3–10)

The replies to Antonio's urgently solicitous requests may be exceedingly well-mannered but they are all 'no'. Rebuffs are no less rebuffs because they dress themselves up in tall tales of stellar influence or Latinate polysyllables ('my determinate voyage is mere extravagancy') which boil down to a statement that he doesn't know where he's going, but, wherever that is, he's going alone. However, *Twelfth Night* nowhere explicitly suggests that this brush-off is an intentional rejection of Antonio. The speciousness of Sebastian's reasoning could only be eliminated if he were to say instead, 'Look here, the plot mechanics of the play we are in require that I should turn up in Illyria in order to be mistaken for my sister who is pretending to be me. You are not strictly necessary to this plot, but to add complications and parallels, it will be a good idea for you to be seen, from the beginning, looking for me, so that in due course you can give me your purse and then, mistaking her for me, make a violent row because she fails to deliver it. So goodbye.' Some of the woodenness of the writing, together with the highly wrought emotion of this area of the play, may stem from the incorporation of elements not perfectly in tune with the overall melodic curve of the drama. The in essence tragic but in execution comic thrust of the relationship brings an imbalance to the play. But that imbalance itself is creative. It jangles the melancholy musicality and grates against the festive rollicks, bringing to the fore the solitaries who have no place in the party-ending. Antonio as an excrescent outsider whose desire is never gratified is echoed by the more low-key outsiderliness of Sir Andrew and Feste, and the 'shan't play' of Malvolio's furious exit. Thus the symmetrically complementary speeches sound a chivalrous and courtly but emotionally problematic rhetoric foreign to the play as a whole, just as Antonio is literally a foreigner and *persona non grata* in Illyria:

ANTONIO *Pardon me, sir, your bad entertainment.*
SEBASTIAN *O good Antonio, forgive me your trouble.*
ANTONIO *If you will not murder me for my love, let me be your servant.*
SEBASTIAN *If you will not undo what you have done – that is, kill him whom you have recovered – desire it not.*

(II.1.29–34)

In this courtesy-competition, each vies for priority in promoting the other's interests. The antiphonal hyperboles produce a curious effect of strained and stressful formality, in which Antonio strives for an intimacy which Sebastian self-deprecatingly evades. The final couplet, uttered in soliloquy after Sebastian has decamped, announces the violence of Antonio's attachment:

> *But come what may, I do adore thee so,*
> *That danger shall seem sport, and I will go.*
> (42–3)

Adoration, even when professed in a sleek couplet, is a dynamic emotion in a play of indirections and proxy-wooings, in which direct protestations of love are rare. This vein of operatic ardour is sustained and even heightened as the play unfolds. Catching up with Sebastian in Illyria in Act III, Antonio protests (in a scene which clanks with plot mechanics) that he could not bear to stay away, thinking of his friend unprotected on a dangerous voyage: 'My desire / More sharp than filèd steel, did spur me forth' (III.3.4–5). His highly charged behaviour is patterned on the protective (but also possessive) benignancy conventionally evoked by the junior in the senior, or the female in the male. Indulgently, he hands over his purse, fancying that his friend might care to buy 'some toy' or knick-knack while he window-shops (45–6). All this solicitous fussing, in combination with a laboured exposition of his historic offence against the Illyrian state, gives a strange image of a man at once driven and covert, whose aggressive maleness is sheathed in tender but difficult emotions.

Like his namesake, the Antonio of *The Merchant of Venice*, who also hazarded 'purse' and 'person' for the beloved, the Antonio of *Twelfth Night* is destined to mateless singleness at the end of the play, a silence in the general harmony of celebratory voices. Like the melancholy capitalist of the former play, who plays the atoning Christ in sacrificing himself for his friend, he too offers himself for his friend, but with sword drawn as he intervenes between the two craven duellists: 'I take the fault on me ... I for him defy you' (III.4.304–5). The startling imagery, which combines Biblical with fencing terminology, implies a self-identification of Antonio with his friend, which recalls the Sonnets, where the projection of the self on to another person involves a life-threatening loss of self should the beloved prove untrue or unworthy. In the Sonnets, rhapsodic idealism about the Young Man's perfections yields to a wrenching conflict with the facts of his fallibility, neglect and sexual betrayal. Investing another man with his own identity, the Shakespeare persona lives doubled and twinned, but also halved. To love is self-love, thus extended:

> O, how thy worth with manners may I sing
> When thou art all the better part of me?
> What can mine own praise to mine own self bring,
> And what is't but mine own when I praise thee?
>
> (39)

The Sonnets are riddled with worry about the dividing or multiplication of the self, fanatically computing on two fingers as to how to live with the uncontrollable autonomy of the other partner. The burden of dependency and disguised demand is a deadly weight both on the psyche and the relationship: the lover is inexorably bound to disappointment and rejection. The insecure mathematics of the Sonnets multiplies ('Let me confess that we two must be twain' (36)); self-divides ('Mine eye and heart are at a mortal war' (46)); self-deludes ('So shall I live, supposing thou art true, / Like a deceivèd husband' (93)); and with queasy cynicism whitewashes the Young Man's betrayals ('O, in what sweets dost thou thy sins enclose!' (95)). At the heart of the Sonnets' all-engrossing passion of older man for younger huddles a chronic insecurity, and separation-anxiety: losses, absences, gaps, rifts, a sense of nothingness and meaninglessness haunt the insomniac lover in the boundless-seeming interstices between meetings, as he watches the clock from one 'world-without-end hour' to its protracted successor. Such self-devouring love involves not only transference but homage which, if spurned, will leave the lover demeaned and mortified. To make another person the vehicle of all good is to commit 'idolatry' (105).

Twelfth Night gives a kind of operatic replaying of these themes, especially in its treatment of the humiliating embarrassment and chagrin of the rejected lover (Olivia's shame at her undignified behaviour – 'Have you not set mine honour at the stake' (III.1.5); Orsino's bale at Olivia's 'ingrate and unauspicious altars' (V.1.111)). But the theme is sounded far more gratingly in the man-boy relationship of Antonio and Sebastian where mortification comes not from loss of face (Antonio has none in Illyria) but the wound to his most private pride and trust. His rage when he believes that Sebastian has publicly repudiated him and surrendered him to prison makes bitter testimony to his depositing of total worth (symbolized by the purse) in another individual – a dangerous once-in-a-lifetime speculation in an otherwise, perhaps, costive and retentive nature. As the officers prepare to manhandle him off-stage, he accuses the youth not only of ingratitude and theft but also of desecrating the holy:

> *Let me speak a little. This youth that you see here*
> *I snatched one half out of the jaws of death;*
> *Relieved him with such sanctity of love;*
> *And to his image, which methought did promise*
> *Most venerable worth, did I devotion.*

FIRST OFFICER *What's that to us? The time goes by. Away!*
ANTONIO *But O, how vile an idol proves this god!*
> *Thou hast, Sebastian, done good feature shame.*

> (III.4.350–57)

In other words, Sebastian has been all face: a neat irony in that the 'good feature' of the youth he accuses is indeed an *image* only, a replica of the beloved. Antonio's frenzy belongs to a worshipper to whom holy things have been revealed as cheap: a trashy boy, laughing up his sleeve, has milked his devotion and valued his purse, that liberally given sign of his own self-giving, but not his person. Antonio's purse is the comic equivalent of Othello's tragic handkerchief, as well as a signal that love may be a capital investment as hazardous as the mercantile misadventures that strike the fortune of that other Antonio of *The Merchant*. With the failure of his trust comes a sense of desecration familiar to readers of the Sonnets, *Othello* and the Last Plays. The poet lays this on heavily: 'sanctity of love' implies the performance of ministrations whose suggestion of deliverance and resurrection recalls the Gospel teaching of the blessedness of him who shall lay down his life for his friend. Antonio presents himself as the Petrarchan worshipper to whom love is a religion, from whose eyes the scales have fallen, to reveal his 'god' as a graven 'image' or 'vile idol'. The timbre and texture of Antonio's speeches incline towards rant, so that the mode remains – just about – comic. But comedy has many mansions, and Viola's 'I hate ingratitude' (345) informs this scene with something of the disturbance that is refined to lyrical melancholy in the Arden of *As You Like It* ('Blow, blow, thou winter wind, / Thou art not so unkind / As man's ingratitude' (II.7.175–77)) and cynically extenuated in the Sonnets:

> All men make faults, and even I in this,
> Authorizing thy trespass with compare,
> Myself corrupting, salving thy amiss,
> Excusing thy sins more than thy sins are . . .
>
> (35)

The subtler music of the Sonnets points up the more histrionic and stylized treatment with which Shakespeare assimilates the smarting insult of ingratitude to a play which insists that it *is* only a play – a juggling display which throws around the only apparently breakable crockery of emotions founded upon delusion and trickery.

In the final Act, Antonio's case against 'that most ingrateful boy' again rings out in a verse swollen to a rhetoric of sublimer rhetorical elaborations:

> *A witchcraft drew me hither.*
> *That most ingrateful boy there by your side*
> *From the rude sea's enraged and foamy mouth*
> *Did I redeem; a wrack past hope he was.*
> *His life I gave him, and did thereto add*
> *My love without retention or restraint,*
> *All his in dedication. For his sake*
> *Did I expose myself – pure for his love –*
> *Into the danger of this adverse town;*
> *Drew to defend him when he was beset;*
> *Where, being apprehended, his false cunning –*
> *Not meaning to partake with me in danger –*
> *Taught him to face me out of his acquaintance,*
> *And grew a twenty years' removèd thing*
> *While one would wink; denied me mine own purse*
> *Which I had recommended to his use*
> *Not half an hour before.*
>
> (V.1.74–90)

Antonio's case against Sebastian is charged with quasi-religious implication. He portrays himself as a redeemer, with suggestions of birth-deliverance ('His life I gave him'), which seeks to extort affiliation based on the sacrosanct ties of parent and child as well as of Creator and creature; he pictures his own advent in Illyria in pursuit of his beloved as a Christ-like sacrifice ('For his sake / Did I expose myself') and rhetorically doubles the alleged virtue of his motives in the amplification 'pure for his love'. Loaded with such a weight of obligation, one may be pardoned for feeling that any slender youth would do well to bolt. The phrase 'a twenty years' removèd thing' is neatly ironic, since it outstrips Sebastian's actual age by several years. This study in curdled idealism swiftly gives way to the parallel howl of rejection and betrayal with which Orsino vents an equal blast of wrath on his 'boy' and his Lady in a three-cornered relationship which faintly echoes the liaison of the Young Man and the Dark Lady of the Sonnets (115–29). Orsino, however, will get his 'boy': for him, the ambivalent 'cheveril glove' of gender will obligingly turn inside-out to accommodate his desire, just as Olivia will get her 'girl'. But there are not enough twins to go round, in order to accord Antonio his heart's-desire, and no place in the theatre, as in the social organization outside it, for primary male bondings – unless you count the first genuinely affectionate words Sebastian has ever uttered to Antonio in this one-sided pursuit as a consolation prize:

> *Antonio! O, my dear Antonio!*
> *How have the hours racked and tortured me*
> *Since I have lost thee!*

(215–17)

After two further exclamations of wonder, Antonio will vanish from the text into a silence which lasts out the remaining two hundred lines of the play. On the page, such silence is a mark of absence from the consciousness of the text; on the stage, it is open to polysemous interpretation. Some productions integrate the silent Antonio with the joyous community of patrician lovers celebrating their good luck; darker readings have tended to interpret that silence as a sign of exclusion and alienation, providing a shadow which sets into relief and brings into possible question the glossy 'goldenness' of the harmonious romantic conclusion. In a play of double meanings and equivocations, silence is the one sign which is fully open to the construction of the reader or director. The playwright, having no further use for the character, has put him to linguistic death: it is left to us to decide what to do with the body.

Montaigne, in his friendly and curious *Essays*, translated into English

132

by Shakespeare's friend, John Florio, in 1595, reports a piece of local gossip which links the fact of gender with the transforming power of the sexual imagination in a manner at once comic and unnerving. This story of sex-change brought about by the natural and universal fascination with sex which produces sexual fantasies is given as an example of the psychosomatic basis of physical conditions, alongside the hysterical tendency of imaginative persons to develop the symptoms of diseases which afflict others, and of terrified persons to die of fright. Prolonged mental fixation on the genitals of the other sex might well bring about a worrying sex-change:

> Passing through Vitry-le-François, I was shown a man whom the Bishop of Soissons had confirmed under the name of Germain, but whom all the village's inhabitants had both known and seen to be a girl, and who had been called Marie up to the age of twenty-two. He was then old, had a heavy growth of beard, and was unmarried. He said that as he was straining to take a jump his male organs appeared; and the girls of that neighbourhood still sing a song in which they warn one another not to take long strides or they may turn into boys, like Marie Germain. It is not very surprising that this sort of accident occurs frequently, for the imagination is so continually drawn to this subject that, supposing it has any power over such things, it would be better for it to incorporate the virile member in a girl once and for all, rather than subject her so often to the same thoughts and the same violence of desire.
>
> ('On the Power of the Imagination', *Essays* p. 38).

If gender may be thought of as psychosomatic, then the imagination has potency indeed. Marie is a cautionary instance of *What You Will*: desire in her/his case engendered the incorporation of the desired addendum. Montaigne, sceptic and rationalist as he is, is by no means ready to dismiss such biological freaks as the gossip of credulous peasants, since he knows from other accredited sources (most authoritatively the testimony of his own experience) the pathological openness of the body's functions to affects of the mind, psychological impotence being a case in point, as well as religious transformations such as the stigmata and catalepsy. Then again there are the common-or-garden reactive maladies which afflict a sensitive temperament: 'A perpetual cougher irritates my lungs and my throat . . . As I observe a disease, so I catch it and give it lodging in myself' (pp. 36–7). He cites the therapeutic effects of the placebo, and notes that the close connection between the mind and the body is observable even in dogs, which pine away with grief for their masters and bark and tremble in their dreams.

For a girl to sprout a phallus might caution most to walk round the puddle rather than taking an imprudent leap, for wishes might come true with unpredictable literality, and in real life the process could not be reversed. 'Germain' *cannot* resume his/her role and identity as 'Marie', as 'Cesario' *can* revert to Viola. Perhaps, indeed, Germain did not regret the death of 'Marie', having become the person he felt he truly was all the time when 'he' was 'she'. But if *he* and *she* are allowed to become indeterminate signs, gender-identity is revealed as a masquerade and sexuality itself a slippery medium in which only the imagination (or libido) reigns supreme. I, the author of this book, am a woman, but there might well be a man inside me waiting to get out. Through its motif of boy–girl twinning, *Twelfth Night* suggests to our easily beguiled imaginations such 'high fantastical' possibilities. For Montaigne, the person he met at Vitry-le-François was to be referred to under both female and male names, as 'Marie Germain', for after all 'he' had been confirmed as a female member of the Church by no less a person than the Bishop of Soissons, who authorizes official identities once and for all. Androgynes and transsexuals, like dwarves, sufferers from gigantism, 'elephant men', those born with no arms, as Siamese twins or with a cyclops eye, have immemorially terrified and fascinated the rest of us as freaks representative either of a divine or a monstrous assault upon the norm. 'Marie Germain' can be safely marginalized as a one-off freak, to avoid destabilizing the social order, but it is notable that not only the local girls with their talismanic chant warning against long strides, but also Montaigne himself, regarded such transformations as capable of 'occur[ring] frequently'. Imaginative mutation is perceived as an in-built function of the natural order. The natural order therefore defies the social order, and all identity comes into doubt. Four centuries later, we can justify Montaigne's open-mindedness by reference to the numerous documented cases of persons convinced from infancy that they had somehow been born into the 'wrong' sex: constructing themselves a transvestite identity, they may later seek surgical amendment of Nature's error. Renaissance judicial reports of comparable sex-changes are almost invariably in one direction: female to male, as if to reflect the medical patriarchy's analysis of the female as an incomplete or abortive male, whose anatomical aspirations towards the privilege of the phallus had been thwarted. Montaigne's maidens feared athletic striding on plausible grounds: scientists viewed their genital organs as constituting a symmetrical outside-in reversal of the males', hence these organs might be jolted into falling literally inside-out. It followed that Montaigne (himself something of a misogynist) need never fear that undue physical exertion in combination with excited thoughts might turn *him* into a woman, since the dangling or aspiring worm of the male member was biology's irreversible highest goal and final end.

In *Twelfth Night*, the beauty of imaginative transformation is that it is a two-way, endlessly reversible process, from the boy-actor to the girl-character, to the boy-character s/he acts. The 'cheveril glove' of gender, softly flexible, turns inside-out and outside-in at one and the same time as illusion melts into illusion, and identity floats free of constraining gravity under the Janus-laws of the double-talking imagination. Freakishness in cross-dressing is doubled by assimilation to that other *lusus naturae*, the phenomenon of identical twins. But paradoxically, that doubling also normalizes the sexual aberration, since identical twins are of common occurrence – although boy–and–girl twins are never identical in life, as they may be on the stage. As the area of the imagination, the stage normalizes and legitimizes all upon whom its light plays: that strange mutation, Viola/'Cesario', speaks to us in a perfectly normal voice and we are soon at home with her/him. Entering the beholder's eye, she fills the space behind the eyes with fugitive and catalysing dreams, like a personification of the erotic imagination itself:

> *Even so quickly may one catch the plague?*
> *Methinks I feel this youth's perfections,*
> *With an invisible and subtle stealth,*
> *To creep in at mine eyes. Well, let it be!*
>
> (I.5.284–87)

Further Reading

Editions

Throughout this study the edition of *Twelfth Night* primarily referred to is the New Penguin, edited by M. M. Mahood (Harmondsworth, 1968). All quotations and line-references relate to this edition, except where otherwise stated. However, students wishing to study the play in detail for themselves are recommended to use the Arden edition, edited by J. M. Lothian and T. W. Craik (London and New York, 1975), with its fuller textual apparatus, ample and scrupulous annotation and its greater closeness to the Folio text.

Criticism and Background

Bacon, Sir Francis, *The 'Novum Organum Scientiarum'*, Dr Shaw (tr. and ed.), London, 1880.

Barber, C. L., *Shakespeare's Festive Comedy: A Study of Dramatic Form and its Relation to Social Custom*, Princeton, New Jersey, 1959.

Berry, Edward, *Shakespeare's Comic Rites*, Cambridge, 1984.

Berry, Ralph, *Shakespeare's Comedies: Explorations in Form*, Princeton, New Jersey, 1972.

Bruno, Giordano, *The Heroic Frenzies*, P. E. Memmo, Jr (tr. and introd.), Columbia, 1959.

Carroll, William C., *The Metamorphosis of Shakespearean Comedy*, Princeton, New Jersey, 1985.

Castiglione, Baldassare, *The Courtier (Il Cortigliano del Conte Baldassare Castiglione)*, Sir Thomas Hoby (tr.), London, 1561.

Davies, Stevie (ed.), *Renaissance Views of Man*, Manchester, 1978.

Donawerth, Jane, *Shakespeare and the Sixteenth Century Study of Language*, Urbana and Chicago, 1984.

Donne, John, *Poetical Works*, H. J. C. Grierson (ed.), Oxford, 1929.

Driscoll, J. P., *Identity in Shakespearean Drama*, Princeton, New Jersey, 1983.

Dusinberre, Juliet, *Shakespeare and the Nature of Woman*, London and Basingstoke, 1975.

Frye, Northrop, *A Natural Perspective: The Development of Shakespearean Comedy and Romance*, New York and London, 1965.

Hazlitt, W. C., *The English Drama and Stage: Documents Relating to Theatres*, London, 1869.

Honigmann, E. A. J., *Shakespeare's Impact on his Contemporaries*, London, 1982.

Jones, Emrys, *Scenic Form in Shakespeare*, Oxford, 1971.

Kamen, H., *The Iron Century: Social Change in Europe, 1560–1660*, London, 1971.

Levin, Richard A., *Love and Society in Shakespearean Comedy: A Study of Dramatic Form and Content*, Newark, 1985.

Lyly, John, *The Complete Works*, R. Warwick Bond (ed.), Oxford, 1973.

MacCary, Thomas, *Friends and Lovers: The Phenomenology of Desire in Shakespearean Comedy*, New York, 1985.

McGuire, Philip C., *Speechless Dialect: Shakespeare's Open Silences*, London, Berkeley and Los Angeles, 1985.

Marlowe, Christopher, *The Complete Plays*, J. B. Steane (ed.), Harmondsworth, 1969.

Maynard, Winifred, *Elizabethan Lyric Poetry and its Music*, Oxford, 1986.

Montaigne, Michel de, *Essays*, J. M. Cohen (tr. and ed.), Harmondsworth, 1958.

Palmer, D. J. (ed.), *'Twelfth Night': A Casebook*, London and Basingstoke, 1972.

Parker, Patricia, and Hartman, Geoffrey, *Shakespeare and the Question of Theory*, New York and London, 1985.

Plato, *Phaedrus and Letters VII and VIII*, Walter Hamilton (tr. and introd.), Harmondsworth, 1975.

— *The Symposium*, Walter Hamilton (tr.), Harmondsworth, 1951.

Salingar, Leo, 'The Design of *Twelfth Night*', *Shakespeare Quarterly* IX (1958).

— *Dramatic Form in Shakespeare and the Jacobeans*, London, 1986.

— *Shakespeare and the Traditions of Comedy*, Cambridge, 1974.

Sidney, Sir Philip, *An Apology for Poetry, or, The Defence of Poetry*, Geoffrey Shepherd (ed.), London, 1965.

Spencer, T. J. B. (ed.), *Elizabethan Love Stories*, Harmondsworth, 1968.

Spenser, Edmund, *The Poetical Works*, J. C. Smith and E. de Selincourt (eds), London, New York and Toronto, 1912.

Strong, Roy, *The Renaissance Garden in England*, London, 1979.

Wilson, Jean, *Entertainments for Elizabeth I*, Woodbridge, 1980.

Discover more about our forthcoming books through Penguin's FREE newspaper...

READ MORE IN PENGUIN

In every corner of the world, on every subject under the sun, Penguin represents quality and variety – the very best in publishing today.

For complete information about books available from Penguin – including Puffins, Penguin Classics and Arkana – and how to order them, write to us at the appropriate address below. Please note that for copyright reasons the selection of books varies from country to country.

In the United Kingdom: Please write to *Dept. JC, Penguin Books Ltd, FREEPOST, West Drayton, Middlesex UB7 OBR.*

If you have any difficulty in obtaining a title, please send your order with the correct money, plus ten per cent for postage and packaging, to *PO Box No. 11, West Drayton, Middlesex UB7 OBR*

In the United States: Please write to *Consumer Sales, Penguin USA, P.O. Box 999, Dept. 17109, Bergenfield, New Jersey 07621-0120.* VISA and MasterCard holders call 1-800-253-6476 to order all Penguin titles

In Canada: Please write to *Penguin Books Canada Ltd, 10 Alcorn Avenue, Suite 300, Toronto, Ontario M4V 3B2*

In Australia: Please write to *Penguin Books Australia Ltd, P.O. Box 257, Ringwood, Victoria 3134*

In New Zealand: Please write to *Penguin Books (NZ) Ltd, Private Bag 102902, North Shore Mail Centre, Auckland 10*

In India: Please write to *Penguin Books India Pvt Ltd, 706 Eros Apartments, 56 Nehru Place, New Delhi 110 019*

In the Netherlands: Please write to *Penguin Books Netherlands bv, Postbus 3507, NL-1001 AH Amsterdam*

In Germany: Please write to *Penguin Books Deutschland GmbH, Metzlerstrasse 26, 60594 Frankfurt am Main*

In Spain: Please write to *Penguin Books S. A., Bravo Murillo 19, 1° B, 28015 Madrid*

In Italy: Please write to *Penguin Italia s.r.l., Via Felice Casati 20, I–20124 Milano*

In France: Please write to *Penguin France S. A., 17 rue Lejeune, F–31000 Toulouse*

In Japan: Please write to *Penguin Books Japan, Ishikiribashi Building, 2–5–4, Suido, Bunkyo-ku, Tokyo 112*

In Greece: Please write to *Penguin Hellas Ltd, Dimocritou 3, GR–106 71 Athens*

In South Africa: Please write to *Longman Penguin Southern Africa (Pty) Ltd, Private Bag X08, Bertsham 2013*

READ MORE IN PENGUIN

THE NEW PENGUIN SHAKESPEARE

All's Well That Ends Well	Barbara Everett
Antony and Cleopatra	Emrys Jones
As You Like It	H. J. Oliver
The Comedy of Errors	Stanley Wells
Coriolanus	G. R. Hibbard
Hamlet	T. J. B. Spencer
Henry IV, Part 1	P. H. Davison
Henry IV, Part 2	P. H. Davison
Henry V	A. R. Humphreys
Henry VI, Parts 1–3	Norman Sanders
(three volumes)	
Henry VIII	A. R. Humphreys
Julius Caesar	Norman Sanders
King John	R. L. Smallwood
King Lear	G. K. Hunter
Love's Labour's Lost	John Kerrigan
Macbeth	G. K. Hunter
Measure for Measure	J. M. Nosworthy
The Merchant of Venice	W. Moelwyn Merchant
The Merry Wives of Windsor	G. R. Hibbard
A Midsummer Night's Dream	Stanley Wells
Much Ado About Nothing	R. A. Foakes
The Narrative Poems	Maurice Evans
Othello	Kenneth Muir
Pericles	Philip Edwards
Richard II	Stanley Wells
Richard III	E. A. J. Honigmann
Romeo and Juliet	T. J. B. Spencer
The Sonnets *and* A Lover's Complaint	John Kerrigan
The Taming of the Shrew	G. R. Hibbard
The Tempest	Anne Barton
Timon of Athens	G. R. Hibbard
Troilus and Cressida	R. A. Foakes
Twelfth Night	M. M. Mahood
The Two Gentlemen of Verona	Norman Sanders
The Two Noble Kinsmen	N. W. Bawcutt
The Winter's Tale	Ernest Schanzer

READ MORE IN PENGUIN

CRITICAL STUDIES

Described by *The Times Educational Supplement* as 'admirable' and 'superb', Penguin Critical Studies is a specially developed series of critical essays on the major works of literature for use by students in universities, colleges and schools.

Titles published or in preparation include:

The Poetry of William Blake
Dickens' Major Novels
Doctor Faustus
Emma and Persuasion
Great Expectations
The Great Gatsby
Heart of Darkness
The Poetry of Gerard
  Manley Hopkins
Joseph Andrews
Jude the Obscure
The Poetry of Keats
Mansfield Park
The Mayor of Casterbridge
The Metaphysical Poets
Middlemarch
The Mill on the Floss

Milton: The English Poems
The Portrait of a Lady
A Portrait of the Artist as a
  Young Man
The Return of the Native
Rosencrantz and Guildenstern
  are Dead
Sense and Sensibility
The Poetry of Shelley
Sons and Lovers
Tennyson
Tess of the D'Urbervilles
To the Lighthouse
The Waste Land
Wordsworth
Wuthering Heights
The Poetry of W. B. Yeats

READ MORE IN PENGUIN

CRITICAL STUDIES

Described by *The Times Educational Supplement* as 'admirable' and 'superb', Penguin Critical Studies is a specially developed series of critical essays on the major works of literature for use by students in universities, colleges and schools.

Titles published or in preparation include:

SHAKESPEARE

Antony and Cleopatra
As You Like It
Coriolanus
Henry IV Part 2
Hamlet
Julius Caesar
King Lear
The Merchant of Venice
A Midsummer Night's Dream
Much Ado About Nothing
Othello
Richard II
Richard III
Romeo and Juliet
Shakespeare – Text into Performance
Shakespeare's History Plays
The Tempest
Troilus and Cressida
Twelfth Night
The Winter's Tale

CHAUCER

Chaucer
The Pardoner's Tale
The Prologue to The Canterbury Tales